CAUGHT IN A FLAP!

CAUGHT IN A FLAP!

Des Parunia

AuthorHouse™
1663 Liberty Drive
Bloomington, IN 47403
www.authorhouse.com
Phone: 1-800-839-8640

© 2012 by Des Parunia. All rights reserved.

None of the patients described in this book exist and any reference to any individual who may feel identified is purely coincidental.

No part of this book may be reproduced, stored in a retrieval system, or transmitted by any means without the written permission of the author.

First published by AuthorHouse   12/21/2011

ISBN: 978-1-4670-0928-7 (sc)
ISBN: 978-1-4670-0929-4 (ebk)

Printed in the United States of America

Any people depicted in stock imagery provided by Thinkstock are models, and such images are being used for illustrative purposes only.

Certain stock imagery © Thinkstock.

Because of the dynamic nature of the Internet, any web addresses or links contained in this book may have changed since publication and may no longer be valid. The views expressed in this work are solely those of the author and do not necessarily reflect the views of the publisher, and the publisher hereby disclaims any responsibility for them.

Chapters

What Happened To Our Profession?...........................1
Africa, The Impressionable Years..............................12
More Tales Of Naughty Teenagers 34
Don't Mess With The Girls..87
My Moullin Memories...92
Nazi-Steve and the tactical crap.............................125
Hooray For Henrietta!...133
The Story Of The Burning Buttocks.......................142
The Grand Slam 147
Tall Men Walk Quietly..157
Story Off The Exploding Toilet 172
The Story Of Mr Reynolds' Bag..............................178
A Typical Day In The Life Of A
    Gynaecology SHO 188
Another Hard Day At The Orifice..........................194
Driving Home For Christmas...................................205
The Case Of The Mysterious Hand.........................213
How Not To Take A Professional
    Medical Exam 218
Come Again!...237

Larger Than Life	245
The Story Of The Green Ring Piece	255
All Mouth And No Trousers	260
The Incredible 'Mr Smooth'	264
The Case Of The Vanishing Finger	270
Crabs On Steroids	273
The Freshly Laundered Cock	296
Dream On	305
The Teenage Colposcopy Cold Coagulation Massacre	316
The Story Of The Secretive Goolies	327
The Clinic From Hell	333
Would You Like To Have Sex?	359
No Matter What I Do	363
Dangly Bits	366
The Intrusive Husband	370
Have You Got A Problem?	374
And Finally . . .	381
About This Book	399
Disclaimer	401
Dedication	403

Chapter 1
What Happened To Our Profession?

Dear reader, this is a story about a young man who went to medical school and through no fault of his own ended up as a gynaecologist. I have decided to conceal my identity and call myself quite simply, Mikey James. I would like to tell you about some of the funny experiences I have had, but just as importantly about some of the marvellous friends that I have made along the way. My story begins with why I felt a need to tell you all about this in the first place.

Are you sitting comfortably . . . . ?

One day I found myself sitting in a really dreary antenatal clinic somewhere in the south east. The first patient in the morning was sitting in front of me with a face as long as a horse. "Good morning", I said. "Ugh", she grunted. "What can I do for you?" I asked as politely as I could. She took a deep breath through her heavily nicotine-stained teeth and then said: "Its doin' my 'ead in."

I looked at her quizzically and asked, "What's doing your head in?" She took another deep breath and said, "This facking baby!" At that point, while I looked at this 36 week pregnant woman with seven other children (all in various states of disrepair), I forlornly asked myself, "What am I doing here?" I refocused on my professional commitment to this patient. "Well, is there anything I could do to help you?" I asked as helpfully as possible. "I wannit owt nah", she blurted out decisively in her combined Swanley-cross-cockney accent. "How do you want it to come out?" I asked, quite taken aback. "Scissorian setchun of course", she said. I queried, "Caesarean section?"

"But you have already had seven normal births. Why on earth do you want a Caesarean section and take all those risks associated with major surgery?" She took a slow pause and looked at me very intensively. "I've seen it on the inner net", she said. "You've seen what on the internet?" I replied. "I've seen everything there is about scissorian setchuns." "What do you mean 'everything' there is about Caesarean sections?" "Well for a start", she said, "I've read that scissorian setchuns are less dangerous to the muvver than having a pissiotomy."

Caught in a Flap!

At this point I felt I was losing the worst consultation battle of my entire career. Here was a woman telling me that the commonest surgical procedure performed throughout the world by literally millions of practitioners every day (using local anaesthesia and a pair of surgical scissors), was now deemed more dangerous than major abdominal surgery, in the form of a lower segment Caesarean section! At this point I had an overwhelming desire to end the consultation there and then.

Unfortunately the National Health Service pays me to listen to these people and to continue as best I can. I really wanted to say that the consultation must close on the grounds that it was doing my own head in! So I did the honourable thing; the same thing that anybody else put in this awkward and ridiculous situation would do. I said to her, "I think you need a second opinion."

Later on that day, while I was having my usual three and a half minutes lunch break, which included the inevitable dried up 'NHS pre-packaged, prepared-five-days-before sandwich, (usually sawdust flavoured), I looked at my computer screen. I aimed to clear my mail box before going on to the next clinic which I'm already late for. On the screen was the usual barrage of e-mails, the vast majority of which I would never need to see anyway.

The ones I really hate are about people leaving their car lights on in the car park. For example one would state: "To the owner of a really tasty metallic blue BMW M3 with soft-top and alloy wheels, please note that he has left the headlights on." Why can't he just tell us the flaming number plate and call it a day?

I continued reading the e-mails and became more and more agitated about their content. It drives me mad to think that so many people in this hospital have got nothing better to do than to send complete loads of drivel through my computer, to inform me about things I never really need to know. I don't give 'a monkey' about whether they are going to test the fire alarm bells at 3 o'clock in the morning on Saturday 15th July. I certainly don't need to know about the woman down in pathology who works in the specimen cut-up room who has lost her black Parker pen. This was given to her on her graduation day and had very high sentimental value: 'weep, weep!'

Caught in a Flap!

I suppose the worst e-mails of all, are the ones arising from the Patient Complaints Department. The patient complaint is probably the fastest growing aspect of the NHS infrastructure known to man. Patients are encouraged to complain about absolutely anything they wish.

The one currently on my screen is all about a woman who is accusing me of frightening her before taking her to theatre to do an emergency Caesarean section. I recall the case well because these things do tend to stick in your mind. She had come on to the labour ward at 38 weeks of gestation with a rock hard uterus, vaginal bleeding and a very difficult to detect foetal heart beat.

I was very worried that she was having a major maternal bleed behind the placenta and was just about to lose the baby. I asked her if she would think about having a Caesarean section as a matter of urgency to save the baby and she had candidly asked me why was I in such a rush! I remember replying that if I didn't hurry she might lose her baby and if she was really unlucky, there was a good chance that she would bleed excessively too.

The essence of her complaint was the abrupt and brusque way in which I explained the situation to her and that I should have given her more time to reflect and think about it, rather than 'frightening her to death' by rushing her into the theatre. "What a load of bollocks", I think to myself as I stare at the line on the screen stating: "When would it be convenient to organise a local resolution meeting with this woman and her family, so that I could explain myself and offer the appropriate level of apology?" I think again to myself, "How low have we stooped?"

I rush upstairs to do the usual antenatal and gynaecology ward round. I remember in the old days that the consultant ward round really was quite an impressive event and to the best of my knowledge most people really enjoyed being there. Oh, how things have changed! I arrive on the ward to be greeted at the nursing station by a gaggle of student midwives, a staff midwife and a ward clerk. "Good morning ladies", I said as professionally as possible. A little chorus of cartoon voices saying, "Hiya, hiya, hiya, hiya", comes from the group of ladies assembled in front of me. If I'm really lucky I can persuade one of them to come with me on the ward round to see my patients.

Caught in a Flap!

I can't remember the last time a junior doctor was in attendance with me, because they are all on shift systems and therefore required elsewhere in the hospital. The luxury of a registrar on the ward round is such a long forgotten memory that it doesn't even bear thinking about. I proceed to the first patient's bed only to find her 19 year old spotty boyfriend lying on it having a quiet kip. I introduced myself to a rather frail looking 16 year old who is some 31 weeks pregnant. She's a well known patient of mine having been admitted no less than 46 times throughout this pregnancy with vomiting of unknown origin.

I tried to point out to the staff midwife that we are trying to run a hospital, not a film set from a 'Carry On' film! I politely asked the boyfriend whether he would like to sit in the chair next to the bed. He replied with a completely unintelligible grunt, which I assume implied the reluctant acknowledgement of my request.

After the ward round I proceed to my theatre list where the latest government proposal inflicts itself upon me. The consent forms have been changed! When I was training the junior doctor obtained consent from the patient and he was able to sit at the end of the bed of his victim and explain to her, very briefly, what operation had been planned. This usually took the form of a three or four word entry on the form. The patient would then read underneath that no guarantee would be given that it would be done by a certain surgeon etc and then she would sign a declaration saying she agreed to have the procedure.

Boy, have things changed! The new consent form usually takes longer to fill in than the bleeding operation itself! There are sections to describe the operation in frighteningly graphic detail and explain no less than three thousand possible side effects or things that could possibly go wrong. It has now got to the point where the junior doctors are too frightened to obtain consent from any of the patients on the grounds that they might miss something. Therefore this task inevitably has now fallen into the hands of the consultant.

After taking ages to complete the form, the patient then takes equally as long to read through everything that has been written, including all the small print and exclusions that so closely resemble a shabby insurance policy from a rather dodgy travel company.

Caught in a Flap!

I make my way to theatres, get scrubbed and start the list. Needless to say, none of the junior doctors in theatre with me know anything about the cases, because they were on their shift systems working elsewhere in the hospital, rather than looking after my patients. I think I'm developing a compulsive-obsessive disorder with regard to the shift system and junior doctor's training. In the old days everything was quite clear.

As a junior doctor you simply worked 120 hours a week in the hospital and you worked for a team. You had a boss called a consultant, you had a registrar or a senior registrar to look up to and if you were really lucky you had a senior house officer as well. You were in a positive environment where you could always ask for help or advice. Your only commitment was to know everything there was to know about all of the patients on a 24-hour basis. You were requested to attend ward rounds and tell the consultant everything he needed to know about the patient. You were required to make sure the patients arrived safely in theatre with their appropriate consent forms and the correct blood tests had been done. Finally you had to make sure that they had the right operation.

All you had to do was go to the clinics and make sure that the patients you saw were admitted appropriately onto the right ward, had the right investigations and ended up booking the correct surgery. Life as a junior couldn't have been simpler and it was certainly easy and uncomplicated for the consultants. Again, how things have changed!

At the end of the day I wearily make my way across miles of hospital car parks, which unnervingly resemble the Heathrow airport 'long stay' facilities. Short of actually having a coach to take you to your car with your suitcases, this could be the real thing! In the old days they used to have this thing called a consultant car park. This was somewhere where you could park your car at a convenient distance from the hospital's front doors, particularly if you were needed in an emergency. It even had your own name painted in the parking bay!

The consultant car park has died a death, along with all the other consultant perks, including the consultant dining room with silver service, the consultant's secretary and the consultant's junior doctors who knew all the patients. I eventually find my car and make a rather tedious journey home through the rush hour traffic. Later that evening, when the children had gone to bed, I sit in my study with a rather large glass of New Zealand Sauvignon Blanc. At that precise point I decide that the joys, trials and tribulations of being a medical student and junior doctor in the mid seventies and then going on to be a consultant 'fanny mechanic' must not be forgotten.

I wanted my two little girls to know what it was like. I decided there and then to record as much as I could possibly remember about all the wonderful experiences I and my friends had, before and after, the day I walked nervously into the dissection room of a London Teaching Hospital Medical School in the autumn of 1975.

Chapter 2
Africa, The Impressionable Years

They say that 'necessity is the mother of invention'. If I dig really deep in my heart to try and decide why I wanted to become a medical student, it was probably because I wanted to impress the 'chicks' out in Rhodesia! In fact I learnt quite early in my teenage years that girls were quite intrigued by the whole concept of gynaecology and were always fascinated to hear what would make a bloke want to go into a specialty, exclusively dealing with female reproductive organs!

I and my two younger brothers had a very privileged existence in having a father who liked to work abroad. We had been brought up all over the world during our formative years. As young as 30 my father was appointed professor at the University in Shiraz. I can therefore remember being brought up by a delightful nanny and not speaking a word of English until I was at least seven years old! My dad had the benefit of marrying an extremely young student nurse called Susan who was only 19 when they met.

Caught in a Flap!

Mum loved to party and their home in Shiraz was very close to the local US army base. Rock'n Roll nights out, going on till the early hours of the morning, were a very common event. My mum even learned to drive in a US army jeep in the middle of the night. The first lesson ended in a deep ditch leaving her with the ignition key embedded in her right knee. Not surprisingly she got round to taking her real driving test some 12 years later!

After Persia, dad returned with our family to England and it wasn't until 1969 that we were off again on our travels, this time to Africa. It is funny how one can remember the first day of a new life. When the aeroplane touched down in Salisbury airport on an early September morning, I can remember the amazing smell of the African heat as the doors of the cabin opened. After a twelve hour flight we were all a little bit bedraggled. We were met by a curious pharmacologist who had the most amazing nicotine-stained tombstone teeth, with hardly any gums and the most frightening smile you can imagine.

He reminded me of those really peculiar nutty professor types you used to read about in children's cartoon magazines. He had an ancient P40 Rover the doors of which opened in opposite directions and my first memory of Africa, apart from the fantastic smell of the heat was Tony, the 'mad professor', hitting the brakes so hard at the first T-junction that my head violently hit the dashboard of his ancient motorcar. My first day in Salisbury was associated with a very long headache although things rapidly improved the minute we arrived at the university house.

My brothers and I were amazed at the sheer expanse of space made available for these houses, with their marvellous multi-acre tropical gardens. We spent our first few days in Salisbury running round the garden pretending it was a race track. It was really quite sad. I was always in the front; my middle brother Hugh was always in the middle and little PJ was always struggling at the back. We used to do literally hundreds of laps every day because of the novelty of all this space. On reflection I think it must have been the most amazing waste of energy, particularly in the African heat. As far as my brothers were concerned, they must have had little joy in never being able to win a single race.

Soon after settling into school, dad did the whole family the most amazing favour by buying a big house with a rather beautiful garden, which was endowed with a kidney-shaped swimming pool. The previous owners of this house had made some very interesting additions and the one that impressed me the most was the construction of a changing room, buried deep within the branches of a wide and thick conifer tree. Once you opened the wooden door you found yourself hidden completely within the dark branches.

They had even managed to install shelves and seating to make getting changed more comfortable. Again the garden was enormous, allowing us to do all sorts of exciting things, including driving a family friend Grace's ancient Mini estate around on the lawn for my first driving lessons.

Looking back has made me realise how the level of parental supervision has changed over the last 35 years. Here we were driving around in this lovely old car with three of Grace's daughters screaming hysterically in the back and my two brothers sitting with me in the front. With all this distraction, we often found ourselves coming precariously close to dumping the entire car and its contents in the swimming pool, especially when I accidentally pressed the accelerator rather than the brake pedal!

I remember stopping one foot short of the edge of the swimming pool while my mum, Grace and a few other friends had coffee on the veranda behind the house. Goodness knows, children don't even climb trees these days, let alone indulge in automotive adventures such as ours.

I strongly recall yearning for a girlfriend while we lived in the beautiful suburb of Mount Pleasant. One day my mum suggested that I should go round the corner and see the professor's daughter and have a chat. I was nearly 15 at the time and when she suggested to me that I should be going to see a 13 year old girl, I thought the idea was absolutely ridiculous!

Having said that, I reluctantly agreed; so put on some reasonably smart clothes and popped over to Jennifer Juniper's house. Jennifer's dad was a Professor of Biochemistry who had a marvellous South African accent and a passion for Italian sports saloons. He was particularly proud of the fact that his Alfa had twin 'carb—you—retters!'

I knocked on the door of their rather lovely two storey Dutch-style house. To my absolute amazement, an apparition appeared before me in the form of a beautiful young woman wearing a purple bikini with a halter-neck top. She already had a perfect figure and stunning gravity-defying breasts! I very apprehensively announced myself and said that I'd come to visit a girl called Jennifer. There was a pause and she said: "Very nice to meet you, Michael. You must be one of the James boys who my mother was talking about."

I nearly died. This girl was not only beautiful, but also about four and a half inches taller than me. I responded nervously by awkwardly asking whether she really was the Jennifer I was meant to meet! I now realise that was a stupid thing to say! Her mother invited me into their cool living room and offered me a cold drink. I gazed out through the veranda doors onto the patio where the swimming pool was.

Some fifteen minutes later I found myself frolicking in the pool with this lovely girl, thinking that I was in heaven. It wasn't until her two younger brothers arrived (both in a very typical belligerent younger brother mood, on seeing a stranger in their swimming pool) that I realised I was crashing back to reality. Having said that, I was able to make a date with Jennifer to see her again and trotted off home feeling absolutely ecstatic about my delicious discovery in this beautiful country.

Schooling in Africa wasn't easy for me. Mount Pleasant school was quite strict and they still had caning as punishment. With hindsight, I think I was probably put into the wrong year, finding myself being the youngest one in the class. Things were very difficult then and I don't think I could really keep up with the curriculum or the standards following my education in England. The other problem with Mount Pleasant school was that it was not multiracial and exclusively educated white children.

Being in this environment made it quite easy to start developing ideas and making comments along the lines of those so typical of countries where white people are in a stronger position. These comments included derogatory names that black people were given, such as 'caffers', 'coons', 'hotes' and so forth. It wasn't long before my parents cottoned on to this and rapidly dispatched me to a famous multiracial establishment near town called St George's College.

Looking back on this move, I think it was one of the best things that ever happened to me, as I had some really happy years in this marvellous colonial-style school run by the Jesuits. My educational needs were still not quite met after I desperately messed up all my 'O' levels despite being in the 'A' stream of the fourth form!

My dad was very angry with my exam results and gave me a straightforward choice of going on to the sixth form with my crummy 'O' levels or starting all over again in the fifth form and doing them from scratch. This meant leaving all my friends and going down a year. Looking back, I think it was quite a brave decision to go to form five, but nevertheless it was the right one. I ended up with the correct number of 'O' levels and an opportunity to go into the sixth form with a view to starting medical school.

I could easily write a whole book about my life at St George's College and all the friends that I made there. I have hilarious memories of the Jesuits and their quirky eccentricities. One of my fellow class mates has written a lovely book about his time in Africa and I will not even attempt trying to emulate his masterful descriptions of what it was like at that splendid colonial style college, set high on a kopje in a beautiful part of Salisbury's botanical gardens.

I had lots of friends in Rhodesia. I think my mum was pivotal in attracting friends for me. Mum got married when she was still a student nurse and was an extremely attractive woman. When she was in her early thirties, it was abundantly obvious that she had a huge fan club of schoolboys. It was not uncommon for kids at school to wait for her to arrive to pick us up before they themselves went home. Lots of my friends at school commented on my pretty mum and many were eager to meet her in person. Some of them tried in vain to impress her. Of note, was a very colourful chap called George. His father had a big Greek business empire selling fruit.

Caught in a Flap!

George always came round to our house in flashy cars which he usually borrowed from his wealthy father. One day he had a monstrous white American convertible, probably a Cadillac, if I can recall. He parked the car on the scorched African lawn directly outside our front door and eased himself out of the vehicle. My mum came out to greet him and I remember him grasping the car aerial and pulling it out to its full length while he draped himself over the rear wing and fin of this car.

"Sue", he said, "do you see this aerial? It's just like my cock." My mother, without a moment's hesitation said, "Yes, George, in thickness perhaps!"

This level of humour that she had really appealed to my friends, particularly the younger and less well-informed ones, who were all going through the same stage of their pubertal lives. In other words, showing a frantic and unrelenting interest in the opposite sex.

Our house was always full at weekends with visiting admirers and my friends. Even the gay chap down the road, who was an active journalist and lecturer at the university, spent much time at our house talking to my mum and trying to rectify the political crisis of Rhodesia, as it was then. We also made many African friends and I don't think it is too far from the truth to say that my mother was under some kind of surveillance by the police because of her very open warmth towards the African people. She had a wide circle of African friends on the university campus and my dad was quite open about inviting everybody to his farewell party, when he left the medical school department, in 1974.

One of the cleaners of the department approached my dad and said, "Does your invitation to 'everybody' include people like cleaners?" My dad answered, "Everybody means everybody." The result of this was one of the most memorable parties I've ever experienced. I can still vividly recall the rather large bungalow set in a huge garden in a leafy suburb of Salisbury with literally dozens of cars parked on the lawn and hundreds of people milling about both inside and outside.

My friend Phil and I were dispatched down to the brewery on at least three occasions to restock with huge barrels of Lion ale and lager. I cannot recall a situation where so much beer was being drunk in such a short period of time. The party started at about midday, went on throughout the day, the night and well into the latter part of the following morning.

My dad lined his beer bottles up against the wall of the living room so he could keep an idea of how much he was drinking. I believe he managed to get round the entire living room by spacing the bottles appropriately. Loads of my friends came to this party, all taking it in turn to do the run down to the brewery to pick up another barrel. Throughout the night there were Africans dancing in the garden and the scene in the morning was really quite spectacular. Many bodies were scattered all over the lawn in various states of post-alcoholic slumber. God knows what our respectable neighbours must have thought on seeing the sight of all these unconscious Africans, reminiscent of a tribal massacre! Remember this was colonial Rhodesia where this sort of behaviour just was not on at all!

It is a reflection of the depth and sincerity of my friendship with so many individuals from those lovely times that I still stay in touch with many of them after thirty five years or so. Up until as recently as few years ago I was visiting Zimbabwe as often as I could to see all my friends. Unfortunately most of them have now been thrown out as a result of the political situation, particularly my farming friends. They all ended up in New Zealand. It's not that I don't love seeing them there. It's just that I feel New Zealand is not a patch on Africa in terms of the dramatic sensory stimulation that comes from the smells, sounds, heat and creatures of that great continent.

I suppose you could say that I spent most of my time with Phil Heath. Phil was known as 'Schmeath'. He was very clever and had wavy blond hair and skinny little matchstick legs. Needless to say he didn't really enjoy sport very much, which was of course a very important part of Rhodesian life. I met Phil at St George's because he was rather intrigued to hear that I had a special tree house built in our garden, so that we could go and have secret cigarettes without being caught by our parents. He also heard about our antics of driving Mini cars full of hysterical screaming little girls around our garden.

Phil came round to my house one afternoon and we climbed up into the tree and sat in our little den around a discarded paint tin, which had about three hundred old stompies in it. Rhodesian life was full of funny words like stompies and scafes and exsay. A scafe was basically a cigarette, but there were load of other names for them including herbs or twacks. A stompie was a discarded cigarette butt. 'Exsay' was a derivation of the Afrikaans saying 'I say' and it was quite common when you greeted a friend to say, "How's it exsay". A penis was called a chop or chiloga or even a tool! Looking back I really don't know what on earth we were talking about!

My main talking point of conversation with Phil and all my other friends for that matter was about one thing: girls! Following on from this, I suppose the next important things that we talked about were cars and motorcycles. Rhodesia had a very unusual culture, where it was deemed absolutely necessary to get your driving licence the minute you reached your sixteenth birthday. Public transport wasn't up to much in those days and you certainly couldn't take a girl to the cinema on the bus! In fact 'transport' as it was called was the most important thing that any young person could have.

If you arranged to go to a party, the first thing your friends would ask you was, "Who's arranging the transport?" It was completely un-cool to arrive at a party on your bicycle. In fact having a motorised vehicle was probably the most important social tool that any young person could possible acquire. I didn't have one. In a desperate attempt to gain some street credibility with my peers and particularly the chicks, I pleaded with my parents for some kind of vehicle with a motor in it, stating that I really didn't mind what kind of vehicle that might be.

Somewhat reluctantly I accepted their offer of a 49 cc Velosolex moped, exactly the same as you see in those classic 'film noir' movies from France of fat little men running around with large moustaches, berets and motorised bicycles laden with strings of onions.

My Velosolex was probably already 20 years old when I purchased it and had less than one brake horsepower at its disposal! With the help of my frantic peddling it could reach a mind boggling 30 miles an hour! Having said that, I was thrilled with it. It was a marvellous feeling to have a motor, a real engine, something you could put petrol in and plan your own motorised excursions.

In an attempt to make it more like a motorcycle I devised an ingenious double seat and even built foot-pegs so a passenger could sit behind me. The seat cover was made from a discarded plastic corn meal bag and the padding, I recall, was crushed straw! The whole concoction was lashed with lots of string. The foot-pegs were made out of cast iron girders and probably weighed just as much as the entire machine itself!

Having a motorised bicycle revolutionized my life in Salisbury. I was able to go to parties at night without having to worry about my parents coming to pick me up, not to mention the embarrassment. My younger brother, Hugh, suddenly started taking great notice of my social activities and wanted to come along to my big boys' parties. He was about 15 at the time and the pair of us would ride around town in the middle of the night on our Velosolex, quite oblivious to the fact that we were probably, if not certainly, breaking every motoring regulation regarding the riding of small mopeds. I'm convinced that on some of our hillier trips through the Highlands area of Salisbury, we could have made much quicker progress if we'd been riding individual bicycles!

The love of motorcycles has stayed with me and the irony is, I promised my mum and dad that the Velosolex would be the only motorcycle that I would ever own. I went on to own approximately 25 other motorcycles over the years, finally ending up with a rather huge jump from less than one horsepower to over 180 at the time of writing! In fact, it got to the point where I owned so many motorcycles that my brother Hugh contacted one of the more prominent motorcycle magazines to come and do a photo shoot and an interview about me. The article was rather unflattering and called 'Ungrateful Gits', ie all about people who had more motorcycles than they could ride at any one time and therefore had to have serious question marks about their overall level of mental stability!

Anyway, I couldn't complain too much because I got a beautiful centrefold photograph of my entire collection from the editor. When my friends all saw it they just candidly admitted I was probably going through a really serious form of midlife crisis!

Caught in a Flap!

I didn't have to stay with the Velosolex too long, because I was eventually able to persuade my mum and dad to let me have a proper motorcycle. In other words, one without pedals! I became the proud owner of a very old Suzuki 50, which only seemed to run nicely if you took the air filter off. Not too clever an idea in a dusty climate like Africa, but anyway, it served the purpose of giving me a lot more credibility and I can even remember taking Jenny for a ride on it. Her boyfriend at that time had a rather nice Alfa Romeo 1600 TI so I don't think she was that impressed with my four and a half horsepower motorcycle!

I was never allowed to take a motorcar driving test in Rhodesia, because my mum said that the standard of driving was dreadful. On reflection, she was probably right. For all the other kids, the minute they reached their 16th birthday they were starting driving lessons and I think I was the only one in my circle of friends who didn't hold a full licence. That did not stop me driving however. One of the amazing things about the Rhodesian party scene was that should your parents be invited to the house next door for a party, you would also be invited to it once you had reached a certain level of maturity. For me this was around the age of 16.

At that time I was allowed to drink and even smoke in front of my parents on the grounds that they thought smoking would probably make me so sick I would stop spontaneously. The idea of letting me drink in front of them was to try and create a culture of sensible drinking. Nothing could be further from the truth! On the first occasion that I was invited to the party next door with our very interesting journalist friends, I can clearly recall smoking the best part of half a packet of Rothmans and drinking at least five pints of Lion lager!

I particularly liked our hostess Lizzie, who was an attractive petite woman with dark hair and ample bosoms. She spoke beautifully with her Roedean accent and was quite posh. Her balding, slightly chubby husband, Peter, was quite the opposite and I can remember one day joining this couple with my mother for a brief conversation outside their doorstep. Lizzie suddenly stopped the conversation and said, "Good God Peter, what a terrible smell. You really should do something about those drains." Peter sheepishly replied that there was nothing wrong with the drains saying, "I have just farted Lizzie." I thought this was terribly funny!

Caught in a Flap!

At various intervals during the course of the party I would repetitiously slip out of the Dutch gable house next to ours and quietly jump into my mum's Isuzu Bellet motorcar and go for a quick drive.

My friend Matthew, whose dad had a magnificent farm in Karoi, was responsible for teaching me to drive. Phil helped me hone my skills when he got his own licence, by letting me have a go in his mum's Corsair. These secret missions in the middle of the night in the Isuzu were quite thrilling. On looking back, I must have been extremely irresponsible. I used to drive over to Jenny's house, or even into town to see Phil. I'd always be back within 45 minutes to one hour and then rejoin the party as if nothing had happened.

To this day, I still can't believe that my mum and dad used to walk past their car, whilst it was still ticking loudly under the bonnet from engine heat and not even realise that it had been taken out. It is even more remarkable that they never spotted any change in the fuel level and probably, most interesting of all, the big cigarette hole in the seat which happened when a fag fell out of my mouth as I inadvertently mounted a roundabout on the outskirts of town!

On reflection of all of these events, I'm sure that I would 'kill' my own children for behaving like this. Speaking of 'killing' children, Phil Heath nearly came to the end of the line on more than one occasion. He was the proud owner of a magnificent Fiat 500 micro car, like the ones you see in the 'Italian Job' film. The Fiat 500 is now a major collector's piece, but Phil did not realise that in the seventies. His white Fiat 500 with a fold-back canvas roof was the most fascinating vehicle that my younger brothers and I had ever seen. We could roll back the roof and pretend that we were in the film 'Kelly's Heroes'.

We imagined that the Fiat was a miniature Sherman tank so we all stuck our heads through the roof and pretended that we were going out to the Flanders battlefields to take on the Panzer divisions. Unfortunately, my mother said that none of us would ever be allowed to ride in this car, on the grounds that Phil was a young kid who had just got his licence and this microscopic vehicle was clearly too dangerous to have a bunch of teenagers in it.

One day we sneaked out in Phil's car and had a marvellous outing. My brothers PJ and Hugh had joined us. We drove back into the forecourt of the Dutch gable houses and we were all standing up looking through the roof doing 'Kelly's Heroes'. Unfortunately my mother was waiting at the garden gate. I got out nervously, to be greeted with a magnificent right hook from my mum, which literally flung me against the side of the car.

Both of my brothers got similar treatment and Phil was left nervously looking out through the window from his relatively safe position in the driver's seat. "Phil, if you get out you get the same", she shouted. Phil drove off rather rapidly with the smell of burning clutch plates trailing behind him!

However we did see him again.

Chapter 3
More Tales Of Naughty Teenagers

When my two little girls were three and six years old respectively, they started to constantly ask me about my memories of all my other friends in Africa. I think this followed on after a spate of watching the film 'Out Of Africa' on our video system at home on at least 30 occasions! This film is still one of my favourites and starred Meryl Streep and Robert Redford in one of Sidney Pollack's best masterpieces. The little girls were enthralled with the scenery, the Africans and the animals. They constantly asked me about what it was like when I lived in Africa. The most important part of my time there was with my friends and the more I thought about them the funnier were the stories I recalled to tell at bed time.

Phil Heath was an extremely affable and friendly fellow when I met him and still remained so even after my mother's offer of violence in his Fiat 500! He also had extraordinary intelligence and I thought that he could discuss just about any scientific matter that anyone could imagine. He went on to university after we finished school and got a first class honours degree in electrical engineering. This is truly a reflection of his brainpower. My fondest memories of him go back again to his other exploits with the tiny Fiat.

Phil's was rebuilt by one of the family's friends who I think was rather interested in Barbara. This was Phil's gorgeous big sister. In any event the car at some point had succumbed to a catastrophic fire in the hands of Phil. He had taken this beautiful girl out for a date. He must have been all of 18 years old and had the marvellous privilege of being allowed to drive and having the use of the motorcar. I think Phil got his licence at the tender age of 16 but in any event he was the only one in our group who had easy access to a car apart from Mark 'Petrol Head' who I'll talk about later.

Phil gave me a frantic phone call one early Sunday morning describing his adventures from the night before. He'd been out with his date (who later became an airline pilot) whose name I can't remember. She had lovely long dark hair and an exquisite figure and looked fantastic in a white bikini. He pulled into a garage outside Borrowdale to fill up with fuel at some point in the evening. On turning on the ignition there were suddenly huge bellows of smoke coming from the engine compartment, as the whole car burst into flames. What followed was complete pandemonium as the fire was occurring right in the middle of a Shell garage forecourt.

The adventure culminated in a massive display of Rhodesia Fire Department's best forces. So from what I can gather the date finished and I don't think Phil saw that lovely girl again. On the other hand the car, amazingly, despite being burned to a cinder was lovingly restored again by one of Phil's sister's admirers and I believe it was once again put back on the road.

Phil had access to a variety of vehicles during the time I knew him, because his mum had a good job in the city. One of the cars was a great big Taunus and the other one was a V4 Ford Corsair in white. Phil always had the use of these vehicles on the weekend and we all regularly ripped him off by never giving him enough money to contribute to the cost of the petrol. We all thought that giving him a dollar or two would cover the cost of the evening's activities, but this was always pitifully short of what poor Phil had to spend, to cart around his little group of parasitic 'piss artist' friends.

Those nights were always punctuated by pulling into any off-licence that would allow us to buy beer at the tender age of 16 or 17. Beer was purchased in dumpy packs which were six small bottles in a cardboard container. We used to find that just one dumpy pack each would probably do us for the whole evening bearing in mind our relatively poor alcohol tolerance.

Our weekends, which were usually just a Saturday night, would be spent touring around the various parties that were on the go in the environs of Salisbury. Salisbury parties were always the same but nevertheless enjoyable. They comprised of a whole heap of teenagers in what usually was a large luxuriant garden with a swimming pool and some kind of disco going on in one of the larger rooms. The crowd was always the same but we always had a good laugh.

The music of that time was mainly from artists like the Carpenters who were very popular with us and of course, all the other 60s' and 70s' bands that were in the charts. Neil Diamond was particularly prominent at that time with his song 'Cracklin' Rosie' and our favourite of course was Rod Stewart with 'Maggie May'. Gary Glitter was right in the forefront at that time with his party anthems and we all used to rock around the clock until it was time to go home to our parents. The highlight of my life at that time, apart from the girls of course, was being able to have my own transport in the form of my puny little Velosolex moped.

Incidentally, Phil also had access to one because his sister had a Velo as well. What lovely memories I have of our Velosolex grand prix that used to take place on the dusty, parched grass bush land just outside the back of our house in Mount Pleasant. These grand prix were really a test of endurance for these puny little motorised bicycles, as the path that we used to go along was quite rough and bumpy and pitted with mole holes.

One of the commonest things that used to happen was the little engines trying to break themselves away from the frame, as the mounting bolts all became loose from the constant buffeting and vibration. Nevertheless we used to go round and round for hours using tankfulls of petrol just to see how long these little machines could last. Invariably Phil would win, because his Velo was not only a lot newer than mine, but had much better compression and quite a lot more power.

I have loads of motorcycle memories from Africa, and it appears that the main motivation any of us had for wanting one, was to impress the chicks! Remember, this was the era when the Japanese motorcycle industry was producing glorious candy-coloured pretty motorcycles that could go extremely fast.

Talking of chicks, one of the best motorcycling stories I can tell my girls is about the lovely Iona Lester. Iona was a stunningly pretty, dark eyed, black-haired girl with very fair skin, which was almost porcelain white. She was so lovely that the Rhodesia Herald newspaper had a picture of her wearing a fur hat on the front page, celebrating some kind of Christmas festival in Salisbury. I was so proud to have a girlfriend whose 'mug shot' was so prominently displayed in the national newspaper.

Needless to say, Iona was another hand-me-down from my close friend 'Muff Balls'. Matthew had this unfortunate habit of offering me his girlfriends when he had found a new one! Nevertheless I always eagerly accepted his offers because the girls were such stunners. Iona was no exception, coming from a respectable family up in Alexandra Park. She had a lovely Scottish mother who was quite tiny and a suave, tall father who was a very successful, prominent business man.

He had a great big Mercedes Benz S class, which I remember vividly and they lived in a magnificent house just outside the botanical gardens. This house was fronted by an enormous oak door, which reminded me of the sort of door that you see gracing a mansion on a typical English country manor. They had a long driveway leading up to big cast-iron gates.

This particular story relates to my experiences with Iona and a motorcycle. The motorcycle in question was a Yamaha RD 200 finished in 'glorious candy-gold.' The proud and very lucky owner was Pete ('Poopsy') Pocket. Pete Pocket can only be described as a complete loony as far as I was concerned. I mean this in the kindest possible way, because he was a truly lovable character, but completely mad! He was a long, wiry, lanky-looking lad who came from a fabulously wealthy family. The Pockets lived on Pocket Hill quite close to St George's College, where we had all been at school.

Pete had an outrageous personality and seemed to be fearless of anything. Even as a fourth-former he had the balls to invite girls into the forth-form common room at boarding school! Common rooms at St George's College were sacrosanct for the pupils. They certainly were not a place where you would ever invite girls, particularly if you were only in the fourth form. The prefects would be eagerly waiting to beat the living daylights out of you, if they knew that you would be breaching this terribly important rule. Pete used to bring girls into the common room and have them sitting on his lap or he gave them 'French kisses' in front of all of the other boys. This was truly outrageous behaviour and made him the talk of the town. He also had this magnificent motorcycle and to say that we were all green with envy is a monumental understatement.

This little motorbike was truly gorgeous and blisteringly fast, especially compared to anything that we could get our hands on. They say some memories stay with you forever because they are so vivid. My first experience of riding a tuned two-stroke Japanese motorcycle must fall into this category. I can remember every second of it as if it happened only yesterday. I don't think I have ever frightened myself so much in all my life.

This diminutive machine, with only a 200cc capacity, felt like a catapult when you opened the throttle and shot off down the road, completely out of control. To say that one's eyeballs felt as if they were being pressed into their sockets, is not overstating the situation. Pete was very generous about letting his friends ride his bike. Retrospectively, I think he must have been absolutely mad to let completely inexperienced young teenagers ride his precious new steed.

Despite my limited experience with the Velosolex, Pete was happy for me to try his motorbike. On this particular occasion that I'm writing about, Iona and I were at a somewhat unusual party on a farm in the middle of the bush, just outside Salisbury. This party was crawling with people and had attracted a lot of attention because I think the parents were not there supervising it! Lack of parental supervision out in Africa at that time, usually meant a great evening was to be had by all!

Caught in a Flap!

Sooner or later I drifted into Peter who, needless to say, had arrived at the party with his beautiful Yamaha. After a few drinks, I asked him whether I could have a little go on his motorcycle. Needless to say Pete, in his usual affable way, offered me the keys and I summoned Iona to the back of the farmhouse where the little machine was parked glistening in the moonlight.

To cut a long story short, I managed to get Iona on the back of the bike and just 150 yards further up the farm drive; I crashed the motorcycle into the biggest baobab tree you've ever seen. The reason I fell off was because I was drunk and going too fast. There was also a corner that I wasn't expecting, plus a lot of sand on the drive that made traction a little bit difficult. Iona was quite badly hurt and complaining bitterly about terrible pain over her elbow. Her lovely party dress was torn; she was covered in sand and had scratches over her gorgeous white skin. The little gold Yamaha hadn't done too well either.

I can remember having bent the handlebars and putting a nasty dent in the front chrome mudguard. The bike was still rideable and if I remember correctly, we were able to get it back to the farmhouse, where I had to give Poopsy Pocket the really bad news. In his usual affable and laid back manner, he took the news on the chin and didn't seem to be at all put out. Had that been me, I think I would have been in an absolute fit of rage knowing that my motorcycle had been trashed by some drunken tit trying to impress his girlfriend. I will always remember Pete Pocket as a really pleasant jovial easy going bloke, who at times, seemed not to be in touch with the real world.

Obviously, I had to leave the party early and take Iona home with Phil. I nervously dropped her off at her front door, just before her parents were due to go to bed and I remember the door being opened by her tall father. He took one look at his bedraggled daughter and said to me in a very firm voice: "I think you should be getting home." The next day, I went round to the house with flowers, to offer my apologies to the family, only to hear that Iona had to be taken to casualty because her arm was broken and needed a plaster cast. I was in disgrace right across the board and even my own parents were very angry with me for my outrageous behaviour.

Caught in a Flap!

About 33 years after that fateful evening with the baobab tree and the mangled Yamaha, I found myself looking in a motorcycle magazine and reading an article about a beautiful golden Yamaha owned by an estates manager somewhere in Hertfordshire. The magazine described exactly the same bike that Pete Pocket had owned, the same bike that I crashed into the tree with Iona on pillion, the same bike that had thrilled me to pieces when I was a very young teenager. At the end of the article there was a small subheading which said: "If you want to own this motorcycle, it is up for sale, please phone the following number." I picked up the telephone within minutes of reading this and a few days later, the little gold Yami was delivered to the hospital on the back of a trailer courtesy of my brother.

I picked her up on Saturday morning after my ward round and watched her being delivered to my friend's house, before being able to smuggle her back to Cabbage Cottage some eight months later! At that time, my wife was not very keen on me having any more motorcycles, on the grounds that she thought seven was plenty, given the tiny amount of space we had at the Cottage! The little Yamaha has a great fan in the form of Arna, my daughter. Arna has adopted this motorcycle and even given her a name. She's now called Yami Annaha and I relish the prospect of seeing Arna riding her around on the university campus, when she's old enough.

Iona eventually had to leave Rhodesia because her family moved and I was very sad to see her go. We saw each other regularly while she was at boarding school in Salisbury. The plan was that she would eventually go and join her family in Johannesburg. At the weekends, mum would drive to the convent school and pick up Iona. She would spend the whole day with our family. These were really good times because we always used to go to the local hotel for lunch. This was called the George Hotel in Avondale and it boasted a marvellous paved beer garden and a terrific Sunday lunch. Most of what I can remember about this place is centred on my dad's generosity, treating us all to Sunday lunch.

We sat outside on a beautiful terrace, basking in glorious sunshine and filling ourselves up with delicious roast pork or beef and having gallons of ice-cold lager. If that wasn't enough, there was always the delicious prospect of being allowed to go home with Iona and giving her a steamy cuddle in my dark bedroom! In any event, by the time we were driven home at about three or four in the afternoon, Iona and I felt pleasantly inebriated.

I was allowed to lie down with her in my bedroom for an 'afternoon nap' without being disturbed by my brothers. I loved those cosy cuddles on hot Sunday afternoons, but I really wished that I didn't have to get up every five minutes for a pee as the result of the four pints of lager my dad had generously bought me. These frequent interruptions were most unwelcome for obvious reasons!

Iona eventually moved to Johannesburg and I made one memorable trip to visit her. This was the first time that I had ever flown alone on an aeroplane and my parents kindly paid for me to fly there on a South African Airways Boeing 707. I can remember this trip vividly, because it really was my first true adventure travelling alone. Johannesburg was terribly exciting compared to Salisbury, because it was so much bigger and more vibrant. More importantly, everything appeared so modern, because there were no sanctions or restrictions on importing or exporting goods. Iona's house was stunning, out in the rural suburbs of Johannesburg.

Her father again had a beautiful Mercedes Benz in a lovely pale thistle green metallic paint. Iona had really come up in the world now and had her own car which was an Austin Apache. This was basically an Austin 1100, with a boot fitted onto it, which made it look completely different from what you could get on the UK market. She was about to start university and was turning into a very confident young woman. I believe that I spent a whole week with Iona and the highlight of that holiday was being driven to a lovely local Italian restaurant by Iona herself.

It was my first real date, if you like, where a woman had actually taken me out. I was driven to the restaurant in her beautiful white new Austin and we had an extremely romantic evening. I remember that we were both very well dressed and the waiter at the restaurant must have thought what a posh little pair of toffs we were. I think Iona was barely 17 at the time, but we felt that we were behaving like fully grown adults. After the meal we had a very prolonged and romantic snog in the backseat of her Austin.

The next day I went to the record shop and bought her the double album by Elton John called "Goodbye Yellow

Brick Road". Unfortunately that really was "goodbye" for me, because when I got back to Rhodesia after that lovely holiday, one of my friends, called Nick, stole Iona off me when he went down to Johannesburg to look at the university! I never thought for a minute that Iona would fancy four-eyed Nick. All he had done was ask me if I knew anybody in Johannesburg that he could stay with, while he was looking around!

I've still got all the teenage love letters that Iona sent to me when she was a young girl, including the one which told me how happy she was to see my friend Nick, who had taken the trouble to drop in and see her in South Africa.

Iona was not the only girl that made an impression on me in Africa. It is true to say that you don't necessarily have to go out with a girl (in other words have her as your girlfriend) to get real enjoyment from a friendship with someone of the opposite sex. I never went out with Angela. I don't think I ever even kissed her, apart from a small peck on the cheek, when she was emotionally upset about a row with a boyfriend, or something similar. I truly adored her and had the most amazing friendship for five years, whilst I lived in Africa.

I don't think we ever held hands or even had a smoochy dance, but I do remember always fancying her like mad! Not having any of the tools to impress Rhodesian chicks with, such as a car or motorcycle, I needed to rely on my future aspirations. In order to impress her I told her of my ambitions to go to medical school and eventually become a gynaecologist! My parents were quite surprised at my affection for this girl, as I honestly don't think they could see what I saw in her.

I met Angela at the riding stables, just a few hundred yards further up our road where our first lovely house in Salisbury was. 'Ascot stables' was the place where I really met girls for the first time. I had been introduced to this equestrian establishment at the age of 14 by a tall, lanky lad called Simon Leadbetter who was at school with me at Mount Pleasant, just near the university where my dad worked. Simon was not particularly good at sport, but was very accomplished at riding horses and his house was just at the edge of the stable's perimeter fence. In fact, if he climbed over his garden fence, he found himself directly in the main arena where the horses performed their dressage and other activities. The stables were run by a very flirtatious bloke called Ian Hogson.

He was so sexy and really did have an eye for the ladies. He was quite a small person with dark beady eyes and long sideburns. He cut quite a fine figure, because his overall physique was very impressive and he was also very good at horse riding. He also had something that we all admired and that was a white Alfa Romeo GTV Junior. This was a particularly exquisite Italian sports car from the early 70s. We were all green with envy to know that this 35-year old was still attracting teenagers like it was 'going out of fashion.' One of his latest 'squeezes' at that time, was a lovely girl called Debbie, who we thought had not even finished her 'A' levels.

Debbie had a stunning, slim figure and rode a horse as elegantly as anybody could ever imagine. She had lovely brown frizzy hair, which she used to tie up in plaits so that her hair would sit nicely underneath her riding helmet. We couldn't understand why she adored Ian so much; when there were so many of us able-bodied young men who were more her own age, all readily available and waiting! Rumour had it that there were certain parts of the stable-master's anatomy that resembled those of a horse!!

I'm not sure about exactly how I met Angela Woods, but it definitely happened at Ascot stables. At the entrance of this leafy establishment, just outside the car park, there was an attractive passageway decorated by an array of delicate wooden arches, covered in the most beautiful flowers and bushes. One would have to walk at least 30 metres along this passageway before arriving at the stables proper and the whole tunnel was covered with chirping crickets and exotic birds. Pretty pink and red flowers with their green leaves made quite a spectacular entrance into the stable area, where the main courtyard was.

For my first riding lesson, I remember there was a very nice plump woman from England, who was in Salisbury teaching the young children how to ride. I can't remember her name, but she was very friendly and I was introduced to the other members of the first novice class that I attended. Adjacent to the courtyard and stable areas was the small training arena, which was basically a rather large circle, surrounded by a high dusty straw fence. The horses would all run around following each other, while the instructor stood in the middle of the circle telling us what to do. To stop the horses going off course there was also a lower inner perimeter fence, which appeared to have the annoying habit of banging against your knees or legs if the horse felt that's what it wanted to happen.

There was also a viewing gallery, where people could watch the lesson in progress from a safe vantage point, higher up the fence. This is where I learned to ride horses and this is where I met Angela Woods.

Angela was one of the few people that I met, who actually owned her own horse. She had a small brown pony whose name was Gambol. Angela went to the Queen Elizabeth School in Salisbury and she was older than I was. This is what put me at an immediate disadvantage! I'm not sure what attracted me to Angela so much, but she had an amazing appeal, which was centred on the fact that I thought she was very sophisticated and clever. I also thought that she was a woman of the world. I say this because she seemed to have a very adult sense of taste when it came to music and life in general.

Of course, the fact that her boyfriends were on average, about five years older than me was also intriguing. Angela had brown hair and wore glasses. She was of medium height and had what I thought was a rather voluptuous figure. Overall I found her very attractive, particularly when she was galloping around the arena on her horse. If that wasn't enough, the added bonus was she had a lovely sister called Bridget, who was a bit smaller than her, but older and also very attractive.

I reckon I was about 16 years old when I first met Angela and can remember the frequent rides over to her place on my bicycle during that time, as I practically lived in her house! She lived in Avondale which was about a mile and a half from Mount Pleasant. Angela had quite elderly parents, by the standards of that time and I always thought that her mother looked more like a grandma. She was my dad's secretary, had white hair and smoked a lot. Angela's dad ran a local garage business.

The house was quite an interesting affair, being one of the few places in Salisbury with a swimming pool that actually had no water in it! She had a garage just outside her bedroom, which was converted into a kind of den for teenagers. This was a dark, gloomy room decorated with slow burning candles and incense lanterns. She had a record player in the corner, which pumped out all sorts of trendy rock music, such as Cream and Uriah Heap. She was very fond of the Moody Blues and similar kinds of adult-type music. This was the first time that I had heard the likes of Procol Harem and immortalised singers such as Janis Joplin and The Doors. I used to love being in that smoky room chatting to Angela with the overtures of her marvellous rock anthems playing in the background. I also loved talking to her sister Bridget who, being older than Angela, added an extra level of sophistication and interest for us young men.

All of this was in total contrast to what was going on next door to Angela's house. Her neighbour was a young girl of about 15, who was unfortunately slightly mentally impaired and unable to go to one of the regular schools. She was basically cared for by her mother on a full-time basis and Angela visited her regularly. What I remember particularly about this pleasant young girl, was her amazing infatuation with all the works of David Cassidy, a very celebrated pop singer of that time. Angela and I used to spend hours over at the girl's house listening to David Cassidy music, while her mother watched over us and made us tea. What a stark contrast to the dark garage experience I was usually having next door!

Angela's other claim to fame, as far as I am concerned, was that she was the woman who introduced me to the world of parties and alcohol. If I had to remember another most memorable party of my life it would certainly be the New Years Eve party of 1971 at Angela Wood's house. This was the first time I can remember being completely inebriated. Up until that point, I think I'd had an occasional beer and had certainly never experienced the feeling of being completely pissed or even sick.

I remember exactly what I was wearing at this party, because I was so desperate in trying to impress Angela. I had a pair of white corduroy trousers and a blue paisley shirt, which was partially 'see-through.' My mum had helped me choose this outfit very carefully from a department store in Salisbury the day previously.

I went to Angela's party feeling extremely confident and within two hours I suddenly realised that I was feeling a little light-headed. The Coca Cola I had been drinking had rum in it. This, of course provided by the delectable Angela. Being a very benign-tasting drink I managed to consume gallons of the stuff and I think it is safe to say, that I never actually made it to midnight to witness the festivities. I can remember being violently ill outside Angela's house, making the best use of the empty swimming pool, as I did a huge 'psychedelic yawn' which splattered the deep end! Angela was an educational experience.

Life in Salisbury was not all about girls. I had lots of interesting male friends as well. Recently, I found myself telling this story as my two little girls sat listening to me in a lovely warm garden in the heart of Stuttgart, Germany. My daughter Arna was sitting on my lap and little Susan was sitting underneath a beautiful apple tree, looking at her two young cousins. "Arna, today I am going to start my chapter about Sparrowfart", I said. She asked straight away: "Why was he called Sparrowfart?" The answer to that question is, because we all had nicknames at school.

Phil Heath was called 'Schmeath' and my nickname was even worse. Unfortunately, I had very curly hair when I lived in Africa and my friends thought that I looked like a scrotum! My mother thought that was hilarious and wrote the name 'Scrotum Scalp' inside my school hat. Boaters, as they were known, were very formal-looking school straw hats, just like those that people wear at the Henley Royal Regatta. My mother wrote the name on the white lining inside the hat. One Saturday afternoon, we were watching the school rugby match at St George's. We were all wearing our best uniforms, including boaters. I remember coming home that afternoon and realising that my boater was missing. Back at school on Monday morning, I was summoned to see the Father Rector, down in his office near the main front entrance of our magnificent college.

I knocked on the large oak-panelled door. "Come in", he said. "Good morning Father", I said to this splendid old clerical creature sitting 'Pope-like' behind a huge desk. "What's your name?" he asked "Michael James, Father", I replied. He picked up a boater from under his desk. "That's not what it says in here my boy", he said dryly. He asked for an explanation of the name inside the hat and I only made matters worse, by trying to explain that it was my mother who had put it there! I'm not sure what degree of detention I got for that gaff, but it was certainly long!!

Sparrowfart obviously came from the surname Barrow and he did have quite a squeaky voice at that time. Pete Pocket, who I have described already, was called 'Poopsy' Pocket for some completely unknown reason. Paul Buck, who came from Austria originally was not surprisingly called 'Fritz' and my other dear friend, Matthew Walsh, was called Muff Walsh, or more commonly 'Muff balls'. Not too surprisingly, the tall and formidable Craig Bone was called 'Nobstand' and Peter Slater, who had metal callipers to support his polio legs, was called 'Slats'. I could probably write a whole book about the nicknames of all the boys at St George's, but I think the best one of all goes to one of the girls who we used to like.

Cathy Bouzannis was a very attractive Greek girl, with dark brown eyes and jet-black hair, who also lived up in Alexandra Park. I don't know how it came about, but Cathy's claim to fame was her marvellous nickname. We decided to call her 'Cathy Balls-Anus'. I don't think she ever realised that she had such a disgusting nickname. I think we were able to keep it secret from her, because we obviously enjoyed seeing her and she was part of our group. I'm not even sure whether we let the others girls into that secret. Apart from Cathy and Angela, the other key player in our little group of friends was a girl called Caroline, who lived near the Mount Pleasant Shopping Centre.

Caroline was a very affable plump girl, who also had an interest in riding horses. I think we all met each other roughly at the same time as Sparrowfart arrived on the scene. Caroline, Sparrowfart, Angela and I were all members of the same riding school at Ascot stables. I have already mentioned this marvellous, cosy little meeting point tucked away in a small leafy patch of land right in the middle of our suburb of surrounding houses. A few scruffy stables housed a dozen or so of our favourite horses and the training ring had a tall circular wall, made of the same straw as the African huts, which afforded us a perfect place for our secret cigarette smoking.

Steve's claim to fame, as far as I was concerned, was the fact that his family also came from England and his mother was a Scouser, like mine. At one point, in the five years that I lived in Rhodesia, Steve went over to England to learn hotel management at a college in Northern England. I think he was away for a whole year and when he came back, he impressed us all with his new wardrobe of extremely trendy 'Carnaby-Street style' clothes. I remember he even had a pair of bright green leather shoes. In conservative Rhodesia, this was viewed as something quite outrageous.

Caught in a Flap!

Steve literally looked like a peacock when he arrived at a party. His long flowing rock-star style haircut, coupled with psychedelic paisley shirts, not to mention his green shoes and ultra-flared bell-bottom trousers, completed the picture. For some reason, we all felt that Steve was extremely experienced with women. I don't know what evidence we had for this, or whether indeed there was any evidence at all! However, the point was that his overseas visits, his training at an English college and the fact that he had extraordinary fashion sense, seemed to suggest to us that he had a way with women! From my point of view, any kind of experience I had with a girl was inevitably shared with Steve, as I was always keen to hear his opinion about what I should do next.

Invariably, whatever experience I described to him in dramatic detail, I always had the impression that he had done the same thing already! Steve was also quite skilful at avoiding the fury of Sue James. Like Phil, he had to duck and dive her clouts. Steve was a victim of an evening when we all got into a lot of trouble. On this particular occasion, at our lovely house with the secret changing room, the Boots' girls were staying overnight with us. The Boots' children comprised

Maxine, Debbie, and Michelle and there was a little baby called Peter, who didn't really count.

We were very fond of the Boots'. Grace was a lovely gentle woman with a fantastic operatic voice and Pete was a larger than life, rugby playing athletic giant of a man who edited a motoring journal. The Boots' and the James' were two very closely-knit families and we used to go on holiday with them on a regular basis, as well as spend endless weekends together. Sunday lunches often used to go on for eight or nine hours! The table was always packed with people eating and boozing. We often used to do sleep-overs, with or without our parents.

On this particular night Maxine, Debbie and Michelle, whose ages roughly matched those of me and my brothers decided that we would sneak out of the house and take a walk to the local service station to get Coca Colas and some cigarettes. We waited for our parents to go to bed and then silently crept out of the backdoor of the garage extension room, which had been turned into a TV-den at the far end of the house. It felt very safe being that far away from my parent's bedroom.

Caught in a Flap!

Needless to say, everything went wrong. We walked out to the service station and found out that we were too late. It had already closed. We crept back again, along a dark moonlit road across the grasslands. I don't think that we were even wearing any shoes. Sparrowfart was clearly disappointed that we had no more cigarettes and just as upset that he didn't have a Coca Cola either. As we approached the gate, we were giggling to ourselves about what a wasted trip that was and planning an alternative strategy, in order to extract some cigarettes.

Sparrowfart was staying with friends of his family just up the road and he was contemplating where he could pilfer some more fags by doing a midnight raid!

Just as we were finalising our plans and stepping through the front gate of our house, my mother leapt out of the bushes with a huge belt and nearly frightened the living daylights out of us. We all got belted except for Sparrowfart, who leapt back onto the road and fled for his life. I believe he didn't have a key for the house and had to spend the night asleep in the back of his parents' ruby-coloured 504 Peugeot. Maxine got another belting from her mother, when she got home the next day. Sparrowfart made a point of avoiding Sue at all costs.

My other point of close contact with Sparrowfart was during a holiday that I'll never forget. The riding school arranged a pony trek with approximately 30 horses, riding out into the bush and heading as far away as a small town called Marandellas. This was some considerable distance. I found the whole thing to be an exciting adventure. I had never ridden a horse more than a few miles and on this occasion, we were expected to ride for up to six hours a day. We were told to take special soft pillows and put them on the saddles to make it more comfortable for our bottoms. We also had to take sleeping bags and were warned about the need to sometimes sleep outdoors or even within barns or stables.

The trip was marvellous. Angela and Cathy Balls-Anus also came along and there was a very cheeky little boy called David Iceberg, who was obnoxious. David lived in Mount Pleasant as well and was about three years younger than the rest of us and extremely naughty. His dad was a local GP, but despite his good background, David had an extremely evil streak. He was constantly playing practical jokes and winding up the girls by tormenting them. If he suspected that one of the girls fancied one of the other boys, he would stir up the whole situation by offering false information to the concerned parties.

This would result in chaotically inappropriate match-making and I can still remember the disappointment of him feeding me the information, concerning the possibility that Angela might even fancy me! Nothing is more disappointing and embarrassing than unrequited affection, especially after you have just made a complete tit of yourself!

The pony-trek adventure lasted for approximately one week and was highlighted by all sorts of excitement. River crossings in quite rapid currents were certainly a challenge and some of the gallops across the plains were truly exciting, especially when all the horses decided to stampede and out-gallop each other. I don't remember falling off my horse, but one of the little girls in front of me got her horse kicked and was then flung off, hitting the ground and breaking her arm.

At night we all used to lie next to each other, telling jokes or stories until the early hours. David would play horrible tricks and leave bullfrogs and giant chongolooloo millipedes in our sleeping bags, or 'fart sacks' as they were known. In the morning, we always had the same unusual sweet brown porridge mixture. I can still remember exactly what it tastes like, although I've never had it again since I left Africa. We used to wash our clothes in the river and then dry them out on the trees.

One morning, I woke up with a big slimy maggot coming out of the skin on my back, because the flies had laid their eggs in my damp T-shirt. Sparrowfart made the diagnosis for me, when I complained of an itchy spot on my back and he then promptly extracted the maggot. Every morning I woke up nervously, expecting to find another one.

Eventually, the riding school moved away from its location in Mount Pleasant, right up to Borrowdale, where it became quite a large sprawling affair. It lost its intimate character and its friendliness. As a result of this move and the journey becoming particularly tedious for me on my bicycle (compared to the little walk I used to enjoy previously), I gradually stopped riding horses. I always stayed friends with Sparrowfart, Angela, Caroline and of course, Cathy Balls-Anus.

During my time in Africa, I had the opportunity of visiting some lovely places both inside and outside of that country. We mainly did these family trips by road and looking back some of the adventures we had were quite hair-raising. I remember one trip where our little Isuzu Bellet saloon had six people in it (four seats) and 90% of the journey was on non-tarmac dirt roads. These primitive roads were horrendously difficult to drive on and were covered in potholes and deep crevices. How this poor little car was not shaken into a million pieces, I will never know. The exhaust system however, did fall off on our way to Shongwen, which was a resort on the Portuguese East African coast.

That particular holiday will always be remembered as the time when I discovered that my head could rotate through 360 degrees, without breaking my neck! The hotel was a great big white sprawling building with its main balcony overlooking the beach and the rough sea. The water was crystal clear and deep blue in colour and there was always a danger of sharks. One day we were all sitting on the balcony having a late morning drink and what struck me about this resort, was the abundance of beautiful young South African girls, wearing the most amazingly skimpy bikinis that I had ever seen in my life. The South Africans were a little bit trendier than the Rhodesian girls and certainly seemed to have a more adventurous sense of dress.

Anyway, on this occasion, as I sipped on my ice-cold lager with the rest of the family, I noticed three South-African beauties walking towards me. I can still remember what colour their bikinis were! The girl that struck me the most was in the middle and she was wearing a purple halter-neck bikini. She had the most amazing bosoms, which were barely being contained by her bikini top. They were like two small puppies frantically trying to escape! She walked voluptuously towards me as if she was a model on a cat-walk. My brothers shared in the mutual admiration of this apparition approaching.

Just as she passed by where I was sitting, my mother suddenly gasped, "Good God, her top's just fallen off!" My head spun round so quickly, that I pulled every nerve and muscle in my neck. What pain!!

For the rest of the holiday I was distinctly uncomfortable with quite a severe neck injury. Needless to say the girl's top hadn't fallen off and it took practically all day for my mother to stop laughing about what she had just done.

The other thing that impressed me about this holiday which was over the Christmas and New Year period was the amazing ability of people to forget disasters. One morning, a young man was fishing in the sea and the water was only knee-deep. A shark came in unexpectedly from behind the reef and took one of his legs off below the knee. Fortunately he survived, but the beach became completely empty for the rest of the day. So much for my dad's reassurance about going to a resort which was shark-proof! What surprised me so much was the next day the beach was full with people swimming as normal, as if nothing had ever happened.

The New Year's Eve dinner-dance was also a memorable occasion. I couldn't believe my luck when I saw, just after we had finished a scrumptious evening dinner, a Portuguese girl with her family sitting on a table very close by. This girl was stunningly beautiful in a lovely, long evening dress and looked about 16 years old. Well charged with copious quantities of New Year's Eve drink, I plucked up the courage to go and ask her family whether I could dance with her. None of them spoke any English and neither did she, but to my amazement the father agreed to let me have a dance. Her name was Paulutia and she was lovely.

We were able to dance for hours and hours without interruption and I still don't know how we managed to get through the evening, without really being able to have a proper conversation. I went to bed that night absolutely thrilled with myself, thinking how I really had got myself a holiday romance. Unfortunately, the next day the bubble burst, when I found out that she told some of her friends she was just being polite. Oh well, such is life!

On another holiday, we were heading out towards a South African game park with Auntie Kath, Uncle Mike and Auntie Mo. We used a Volkswagen Kombi people-carrier, complete with chauffer. This poor little 1700cc bus had to lug our large family around the mountains, down into the valleys and across some extraordinarily bad roads to get to the Game Park. Part of the journey took us through Portuguese territory and at one point in the afternoon; we stopped for lunch in a very remote and isolated little village. This one-horse-town had literally one café bar to its name, which was serving lunch. We sat in this scruffy little restaurant, probably eating piri-piri chicken and chips and after lunch we asked mum if we could go for a walk.

The purpose of our mission, for my brothers and I, was to get to explore the Portuguese shops to see whether we could procure any of the famous cigarettes we'd heard about at school. They were ridiculously cheap at 3 cents a packet. Mum and dad told us that we could go as long as we didn't walk too far, so staying reasonably near the restaurant. We found a scruffy little shop and, needless to say, identified the incredibly cheap merchandise. We bought as many packets of the horrible little brown cigarettes (full of stalks rather than tobacco leaves) as we could afford and stuffed them inside our underpants.

I can still remember how uncomfortable it was trying to stow these stubbly little packets inside our pants. We retreated into the bush, as far as possible away from the restaurant, to enjoy our merchandise. We had a leisurely smoke out in the bush and then suddenly realised that we were lost. It took us ages to work out which way to get back to the restaurant and when we finally arrived, the whole of our family was standing outside the van looking bewildered and wondering where we had been. "Hit them Jim!" said Sue in her usual manner, when we had been extremely naughty.

We all climbed into the van with thick ears and continued our journey to the game park. Joseph, the chauffer, was very obliging in allowing us to hide our liquorice flavoured cigarettes in his sealed Tupperware lunch containers inside his van.

It is strange that the variety of friends I had in Africa were all so different from one another. One in particular was never really part of our 'gang' as such, but was very close to me and my family. This is the chap with the car aerial! 'Noddy' was the nickname given to my good friend George, who I've already mentioned. He was a larger-than-life character who couldn't keep his eyeballs still so he used to have to nod his head from side to side. He came from a very wealthy Greek family who specialised in providing fruit and vegetables to the retail market. He had a firm, stocky build and was an excellent basketball and rugby player.

We always felt that he was a little overshadowed by his brother whose name was Mano, but we used to call him 'Main Own'. In Rhodesia if you were a good bloke you'd be called a good 'Own' if you were a bad bloke you would be called a shit 'Own'. The 'Main Own' obviously was somebody very important. Main Own was the head boy of a large high school in Salisbury, which was one of our greatest competitors on the rugby front. He was also the captain of rugby and a superb athlete generally. I always got the feeling that George was constantly trying to keep up with his older and very successful brother. From my point of view, I felt extremely uncomfortable about Mano, because of the fact that he was dating the current love of my life, Jenny.

Just before going on holiday to South Africa, I was able to ask Jenny to go out with me and she agreed to be my girlfriend. When I returned three weeks later, I found out that she was already going out with Mano. With his good looks, sporty personality, success at school and the fact that he had his own car, I didn't stand a chance!

George and I spent a lot of time together. Although he wasn't really part of our usual crowd of Sparrowfart, Phil Heath, Mark Tawnton, Muffballs and the girls, he did seem to visit us quite a lot on a kind of solitary basis. He got on very well with my mother and my dad loved watching him play rugby for the college. He was really quite a ferocious player, who would fling himself dramatically over the line when he was scoring a try. He also had a reputation for exaggerating things, a little bit like me in fact.

Everything he described or did appeared to be larger than life. He was very generous, but equally eager to impress people at all times. There is one story about George which my best friend Phil was very eager for me to describe. Phil says this was one of the funniest things that he had ever seen in his life. The event in question took place on a hot afternoon during one of my visits back to Rhodesia, after I'd qualified in medicine.

I'd left the country six years previously, but always stayed in touch with George, who used to come and visit me in England. I'd been having lunch in his flat somewhere near the centre of the city and had had the opportunity to meet his new girlfriend, who I believed he was intending to marry. Phil had also been invited for lunch and was given a hard time by George, about the quality of accommodation that he was offering me in his mess in Avondale. After a very enjoyable lunch, the conversation turned round to the concept of settling down, getting married and so forth. Then I commented on my recollections of the Greek community being quite tight knit in Rhodesia. I was reminiscing about all the afternoons I was taken down to the Hellenic sports club as a school boy, when George would entertain me with snooker and Lion lager in the exclusive Greek country club environment.

The conversation continued along the lines of this close Greek community, which seemed to mix very little with any of the other people in Salisbury and then I made my terrible gaff. "George," I said inquisitively, "what happens if a white guy wants to go out with a Greek chick?" There was an agonising silence. Phil promptly choked on his dessert and had to leave the room. He says it was one of the funniest moments he's ever experienced in his life, as George dropped his wine glass and the Greek 'princess' shot me a glare that would have incinerated most mere mortals! How dare I question her melanin content!

George's colourful lifestyle continued after we'd all left Africa. There is a terrible rumour that he'd left his Porsche car at the airport in Johannesburg, with the keys still in the ignition, as if something terrible had happened to him. For years and years, nobody had heard about George, but recently I discovered that he has been tracked down to Canada where, unsurprisingly, one of his activities is coaching a female football team!

'Pretty boy' Muffballs will always be remembered as the good-looking one in our group. In fact my mum thought that he was so pretty, that we called a girl who looked a bit like him, Muffina! My friendship with Matthew started at St George's College, where he was a boarder with his three brothers. Like me, he was the oldest sibling. I used to bring sticky buns for break-time at school and shared them with Matthew and Sparrowfart, as they were the two boarders I knew there. On Sundays, during exiat days, Matthew's family were very happy for him to come and spend the day with us at Pendennis Road. Sometimes he'd be joined by his entire complement of brothers. Exiat Sunday started at 10 am and finished at four pm so we only had 6 hours to get through the important activities of trying to find as many girls as possible.

It was good having Matthew on board because, as he was so good looking, he used to attract the chicks. Our group of friends comprised Angela, Cathy Balls-Anus, Caroline and of course any of the girls that Matthew knew already from his previous liaisons. Mark often used to join the group and, needless to say, Phil was always there with Sparrowfart. Sometimes the family would take us all the way out to Mazoe (where they grow oranges) where there was a marvellous hotel called, funnily enough, the Mazoe hotel. This had a sprawling patio-style garden going down what looked like a little hill.

There was a small patio area next to the bar where a small band could perform. I have very vivid memories of the live music and the dancing going on after we had all finished our Sunday lunch. The song 'Sugar Sugar' was particularly well sung by this little group and it almost sounded like the real record. This tiny little hotel in the middle of orange growing country was the only venue at which I have ever experienced the concept of after-lunch dancing on a Sunday afternoon.

Matthew's other claim to fame was the farm. The Walsh family had a huge tobacco farm up in the area of Karoi, heading out towards Kariba. I visited this farm on numerous occasions during my time in Africa and this is the place where I learned how to drive and how to ride a motorcycle.

I can safely say that it was Matthew Walsh who got me on the road to becoming a 'petrol head'. The Walsh's lived in a large bungalow—style house on this enormous farm.

As well as tobacco they also had cattle and grew other crops. The farm had a network of dusty roads traversing it. These were perfect for an amateur like me to learn how to drive a car or ride a motorcycle. Matthew's dad, Peter, a small man with an enormous sense of presence, was married to a tall, slim woman called Joyce. Joyce was quite strict and smoked Rothmans King Size. She also had a smokey voice. Matthew had three younger brothers called Connell, Nick and Stephen.

He only went home on school holidays and regularly invited me along, as a companion for the long vacation. The farm truck was an ancient Peugeot 303, which was grey and battered and had a gear change on the steering column. The motorcycle, which I found more interesting, was a Greaves model with a leading link front suspension and looked like it had been designed as a trail bike. It had a single cylinder, a high exhaust pipe and it was finished in pale blue. Matthew also had access to a Matchless motorcycle from the late 50s, which was a great big black brute of a machine with a single cylinder.

I will never forget hurtling down those gravel roads at great speed with neither goggles nor crash helmets to protect us! Matthew used to ride like a maniac and frightened the living daylights out of me. Our daytime activities usually centred on riding the motorcycles into Karoi and picking up packets of 'Rembrandt van Rijn', exclusive cigarettes from the local hardware store. We would then head into the bush and sit on rocks shooting lizards with a 2.2 calibre rifle, whilst we had a leisurely cigarette, out of the packs we'd obviously hidden in our underpants.

In the evenings, we used to watch the marvellous spectacle of Joyce having her pre-dinner drink. All the men were ordered to have a bath immediately the sun was starting to set and then we would retire to the living room only to see Joyce sitting there in her evening clothes, with her arm outstretched holding a tall glass and saying, "Matthew, be a darling and recharge my glass." At this point, Matthew would spring up like a coil leaping into the air ready to attend his mother. Phil used to find this whole thing quite hilarious.

The family also owned an enormous yacht which they kept on Lake Kariba. Remarkably, the hull was made from cast concrete. Matthew and his dad were quite accomplished sailors and used to win many of the competitions in this large vessel. Another thing that interested me about the family was the Mercedes Benz that Peter had. There always was a large Merc in the Walsh family and what intrigued me most, was that Matthew was allowed to drive a brand new, six cylinder two and a half litre Mercedes saloon.

Caught in a Flap!

He brought it round to our house in Bargate one afternoon and I couldn't believe that he had been entrusted with this beautiful beige car with blue seats. I was so taken with the Mercedes Benz at that time, that I always promised myself one when I grew up. One memorable journey with Peter was returning to Salisbury from the farm, after a big stone had gone into the windscreen of his beautiful car.

We made the whole journey without any windscreen glass. It was quite peculiar that after a while, especially if you were wearing sunglasses, you didn't notice the draft too much. Other memories of my time on the farm are humorous and include the day when Matthew and I were standing in his bedroom, trying to work out what plans we should be making for the evening. His mother casually walked into the room, while Matthew was standing there completely naked and just carried on talking to him as if nothing had happened. I wondered why she hadn't even bothered to knock! He looked a bit cheesed off! I just looked relieved, because I happened to be wearing my underpants!

We regularly went into Karoi at night to the local hotel that there was in this one-horse-town. I can remember getting terribly pissed during cinema nights, when a projector was put outside on the patio and the locals would come to the hotel and watch the latest film on offer. Matthew used to frequently drive us back to the farm with one hand over his eyeball, because he was seeing double so badly! There was no breathalyser in those days!

They say some smell memories remain with you forever. I can still remember the smell of the tobacco barns as if it was yesterday. The smell of curing tobacco is absolutely delicious. Matthew's dad had started the farm from scratch and expanded it to a really enormous enterprise. The tobacco barns were absolutely huge and there were loads of them. The sorting-shed area was like a great big aircraft hangar. The quality of the tobacco was so good that it regularly fetched top money at the tobacco sales in Salisbury.

Matthew's dad was a very hard-working farmer who ran a very tight ship. He was a typical charming 'English-gentleman-type' person, but with quite a fiery temper if the workers started to mess about. I used to watch him give them a jolly good telling off with plenty of f-ing and blinding included, only finding him say at the end of it, "I do apologise for that, Michael."

Over the years as the farm expanded despite the war, the Walsh's continued to prosper. Matthew and his youngest brother Steve both stayed on to look after the farm with their dad, each building their own homes on the land. They both got married and had lovely families. Nick, the middle brother, stayed in South Africa and poor Connell, the other middle brother, died tragically in the early 80s. Joyce never really got over that. Unsurprisingly, just like all the other farmers in that area, the Walsh's eventually lost their farm and emigrated to New Zealand.

Matthew was not the only pal that had a major motoring influence on me. What sticks in my mind about my friend Mark Tawnton is the fact that I thought his parents were his grandparents! For some reason Mark's parents were incredibly old and his mother looked frail, as well as old although his father looked much fitter. Mark was an only child. He was not particularly spoilt though, but he did get some pretty marvellous presents from his parents.

As a schoolboy, he was allowed to have a brand new Honda S70 motorcycle, which looked very smart in black and chrome. This bike was surprisingly nippy for its size and we were very envious of him.

He also had direct access to an absolutely immaculate Volkswagen Beetle, which was the usual Volkswagen blue colour. His dad was meticulous about maintaining this car and it always looked absolutely perfect. Mark used to thrash the living daylights out of the engine and used to impress us all with his fast driving. All of this out of about 30 horsepower! Mark lived in an immaculate bungalow just on the outskirts of Mount Pleasant. It was adjacent to extensive grass land quite close to a small shopping centre and service station. This was an easy bike ride from Pendennis Road and I used to drop in to see Mark quite often. His house was always scrupulously clean and his mother always offered me tea and biscuits in a very traditional British manner.

One of our favourite pastimes was talking about motorcycles in his bedroom. He had a massive poster displaying all the current Honda models. We were both particularly fond of the single cylinder Honda CB125.

Caught in a Flap!

Needless to say, later on in my life I was able to find one of these machines, which first went to my brother, Paul and then did an enormous length of service on behalf of my dad, who used to ride it to work everyday when we lived in Liverpool.

Mark impressed us all when he moved up a notch in the motorcycle world by selling his Honda 70 and purchasing a massive BSA motorcycle, which had a red and chrome petrol tank. Standing next to my puny little Suzuki 50 on our drive at Bargate, this machine looked totally enormous. Fortunately, Mark had quite a tall, lanky frame and was able to handle this machine very comfortably. I can clearly remember him thundering out of our driveway, with his shock of black hair being blown carelessly into the wind as he vanished into the distance.

One afternoon he pulled into our drive, having come all the way back from Kariba, with a massive oil leak from his motor cycle's engine. His jeans were completely soaked in black oil and he told me that he had pulled into every service station between Salisbury and Kariba, to top up the oil from this catastrophic leak.

Mark was a very macho kind of chap and went on to join the Rhodesian light infantry at the time of the war. My mother cried when she saw the picture of him standing there holding a rifle in a burnt out African village.

My fondest memory of Mark has to be the sight of him leaving the George Hotel in the middle of the night with no clothes on and then getting into his car and driving off. It was our farewell night before leaving Rhodesia and the boys had all come upstairs to say goodbye to mum. I can't remember why Mark had no clothes on in the first place, although he did try to leave the hotel with a towel around his waist, but in the hotel lobby they asked him to give it back. He casually obliged and strolled out of the lobby completely naked!

I saw Mark in England when I was a medical student and he came over with his fiancée. I believe they emigrated to South Africa and I haven't seen him since.

Chapter 4
Don't Mess With The Girls

Life in Rhodesia as a schoolboy was generally pretty good indeed. The down side, of course, was the constant struggle with examinations. There was quite a competitive atmosphere at St George's College, particularly when it came to the 'A' level season.

I read nowadays that the standard of 'A' levels has dropped considerably and I am quite sure that is the case. All I can remember about 'A' levels was just one monumental struggle. I have done lots of examinations since then and have never had to swot as hard as I did in those days. However, there were always moments of light relief even during the middle of the intense swotting season, which unfortunately was when the temperatures in Africa were at their highest. On one occasion, I remember taking a break from the relentless swotting and having lunch. My two younger brothers were there, although they did not have to swot because they were not in the middle of important examinations.

Des Parunia

My mother was in a particular jovial mood that day and she was making one of our favourite lunches. Hugh, my middle brother, was in a slightly contrary mood and did not appear to have his usual huge appetite. I think he might have been feeling a bit queasy from the party he had been to the night before. Anyway, mum came up to him and asked, "Do you fancy a chop?" He turned around and said sarcastically, "No thank you, I've got one already". So my mum, as quick as lightning said, "Do you fancy a bigger one then?"

One of the joys of the swotting season, particularly when you were a boarder, was that if you had a good relationship with the head of physical education, you could persuade him to let you go on cross-country runs by yourself. This was viewed as a way of relieving the tedium and monotony of swotting and was considered a healthy activity. Our head of physical education was called Pete Turner, who was extremely good-looking and reminded us a bit of James Bond. He was dark, tanned and very athletic. Mr Turner allowed Matthew and me to go out for cross-country runs in the Botanical Gardens, which were right next to our school grounds.

These gardens were spectacular with huge boulders on them, deep bits of jungle, rather large stretches of savannah grass and mixed vegetation, really representative of all aspects of the African environment.

The big thrill of these gardens, from our point of view, was the excuse to see our friends Angela, Caroline and Cathy. Angie Woods was a lovely girl and a close friend of mine. As I have said before, she was about six months older than me and I never got the chance to go out with her, because I think she viewed me as just a little kid. She had boyfriends that were much older than us, but nevertheless still enjoyed our company. Along with her friend Caroline (who was slightly rotund, but very pleasant) and Cathy, we all used to get together and have great fun.

We boys used to run across the gardens to find a secluded area near some balancing rocks and meet the girls for cigarettes and picnics. I remember that on some occasions, we even had small bottles of beer called 'Dumpies'. All of this was extremely illegal and very naughty and if we had been discovered, I am sure we would have been expelled. Nothing ever happened on these missions, from the point of view of making any contact, such as snogging etc. We simply had really good conversations and a great laugh.

However, our exploits, as far as the senior boys at the school were concerned, were viewed very differently, bearing in mind that this activity started when we were doing our 'O' levels and went on all the way through to doing our 'A' levels. In other words, whenever there was a swotting season, we would be out in the Botanical Gardens. Understandably, the senior boys were quite intrigued about our activities. This led to some degree of exaggeration by us in order to try and show off in front of our senior peers.

I made the fatal mistake of embellishing our stories to the extent that it sounded as if the three of us were in the Botanical Gardens having frantic and frivolous sexual activity with these three lovely girls. Of course, this bit of unfortunate information got back to the girls. I remember coming back to school one dark evening and being summoned to a little Mini Clubman, parked just behind the tuck shop. I was then asked to explain myself in front of three truly livid girls about how I could possibly have had sexual intercourse with all of them in the Botanical Gardens in one afternoon! Here I was, ambushed and helpless in front of them with no chance of offering any kind of reasonable explanation. After all, I could not say that the senior boys had made it all up, otherwise I would have to 'face the music' with them! I found myself in a terrible situation with the prospect of losing my lovely friends. I was in disgrace and felt truly embarrassed. I just managed to redeem myself with a rather wimp and tearful apology!

Chapter 5
My Moullin Memories

If I ask any of my contemporaries from medical school what they thought was the highlight of my medical school life, they would invariably say my marvellous years living in the Moullin Memorial Hostel, Mount Park Road, Ealing W5. To this day, the building exists in exactly the same form as it was when I arrived there in the glorious autumn of 1975. For some strange reason, all the autumnal-orange leaves seemed to be surviving much longer than usual in the hostel's splendid garden. There was a beautiful row of old oak trees, resplendent in their bright yellow and orange foliage, having lost hardly any leaves, even though it was mid-October.

How I ever ended up living in such blissful student accommodation, I will never know. It must have been a quirk of fate, as I believe that my mum had tried to find me somewhere to live in London as a student and had come up with the Moullin Memorial Hostel more or less as a last resort. I say this because the building appeared to be designated for the use of young girls and a few boys from the Royal Ballet School. There was no definite association with the University of London or the need to accommodate other students. The building itself was quite a splendid piece of architecture, which included at least fifty inmate rooms spread over three floors. It had a very handsome frontage, with a nice patio leading onto a splendid green lawn, fronted by the oak trees that I have already mentioned.

To gain access, there was a rather large oak door that still remains in exactly the same condition today. The rules of the house were quite simple. Nobody was allowed to have locks on their doors and each inmate had their own room, but I believe a few girls might have shared slightly larger accommodation. We left all our property and belongings in our room, with the understanding that there was a feeling of trust amongst all of us. No one would enter or leave anyone's rooms without permission and certainly nothing would be stolen. A lovely old housekeeper, called Beryl, was responsible for our floor and used to be like a second mother to us during times of difficulty or loneliness.

I remember my first day at the Moullin Memorial Hostel so clearly. I was thrilled with the anticipation of living in London, having just moved out from Liverpool, after my brief experience at Southport technical college. I had been re-sitting my chemistry 'A' level so that I could get into medical school. I remember being dropped off by my mother and finding myself in this small cell on the second floor. I was quietly excited about my new accommodation, as I enjoyed the smell and the atmosphere of this large house.

I was equally thrilled at the prospect of living with such a large number of beautiful ballet dancers, some of whom I could not help noticing when I arrived. There were a handful of medical students allocated to a few rooms at the hostel. In addition to that, there was quite a nice mixture of a few other individuals, including a small selection of students from various other specialties. These included electrical engineering, the arts and mathematics.

There was even an apprentice street cleaner living in one of the rooms. His main claim to fame was that he was quite a serious sperm donor at the local sperm bank! It is hard to believe that this canny little chap with a wiry frame and dreadful teeth was a popular donor of sperm. He regularly attended the clinic to supplement his meagre apprentice income as he learned his trade.

There were lots of lovable characters in that hostel, but in particular there is one who will stick in my mind for his famous 'one liners'. I first met him on a cold, autumnal Saturday afternoon in Ealing. I had just finished unpacking my case and was comfortably perusing my new accommodation, wondering where to put up my Brigitte Bardot posters.

I hadn't met anybody formally as yet, but I had noticed one of the teenage ballet dancers called Debbie, walking up the first flight of stairs with her belongings. She was also embarking upon a new life in London and with her tall statuesque frame, blonde hair and striking blue eyes, was destined for a career with the Royal Ballet. She gave me a slightly sarcastic acknowledgement of my existence, when I bumped into her for the second time on the staircase, as we travelled up and down with our luggage. "Oh not you again," she had said.

I remember feeling a bit put out, but at the same time feeling that she might actually be interested in me!

Des Parunia

There was something in the way that she'd looked at me as we passed on the staircase.

I stepped out into the corridor deciding that I should really explore the establishment in further detail. Approaching me down the corridor was a slightly lanky lad, with very flared bell-bottom jeans and a distinctive 70's haircut, which made him resemble the famous motorcyclist of the time, Barry Sheene. He had a denim shirt on and a thick black belt. Our eyes met in the corridor and he said, "Hi, I'm noo," in a quite broad cockney accent. I rather unkindly replied saying, "Hi, I'm Mike ! Nice to meet you, Mr New!" I took an instant liking to this lad (whose name turned out to be Andy) but I'm very sad to say that our friendship didn't hold as long as it could have done.

Unlike any of my other close friends from the Moullin hostel, I'm unable to tell you much about what happened to Andy, apart from knowing that he eventually became a GP, having married a pretty girl from up North, who was also in our year. I really did enjoy some extremely good fun times with him and we had some marvellous laughs together, some of which were truly at his expense, because he had no idea about how funny he was!

I joined the Moullin hostel, fresh in a new relationship with a very pretty 16 year old girl from Liverpool, called Ruth. She was gorgeous with a dazzling smile and amazing figure. In fact I was convinced that her beautiful breasts were filled with helium, as they appeared to completely defy gravity! Sadly our relationship was going to be strained, by the rather large travelling distance and expense involved, with keeping such a friendship going.

Eventually our relationship dwindled as Debbie, the dancer I'd met on my first day, expressed more interest in me. As my relationship with Debbie developed, Andy always seemed to be there. I can remember lovely evenings with the three of us all chatting together in my little room, having a beer or two and a laugh.

Debbie appeared to be acutely conscious that Andy was overstaying his welcome and never giving us enough time to be together. She would often say things like "Haven't you got a home to go to?" or "Isn't it past your bedtime yet?" Andy was delightfully impervious to these sarcastic rebukes and continued his conversation with us regardless.

Eventually Andy met another lovely ballet dancer called Helen who had the most amazing shock of red hair. With the development of that relationship, he gradually drifted away from Debbie and me and we didn't see quite so much of him. However, he stayed in close contact as my next-door neighbour in the corridor and of course, as a regular drinking companion at our marvellous pub called the 'Wheat Sheaf', which still remains to this day.

This place was brilliant, because it was one of the few pubs in the area where you could get a pint of Fuller's ESB on draught. 'Extra Special Bitter' still remains one of the strongest you can drink and has the most amazing kick. It is very difficult to drink four pints without feeling completely sloshed. Even when seasoned drinkers from Rhodesia came over to see me, they were always shocked by the intense potency of this brew. On many occasions, I remember dragging them home, putting them to bed and then consoling them the next morning about their dreadful hangovers.

Caught in a Flap!

Other notable friends apart from 'Hi-I'm-noo' were Pete and Sue, who were also medical students. Pete was extraordinarily young to be at medical school and I can remember him looking like a spotty teenager, rather than a young adult. He had amazing blonde hair and was very good looking. Sue was a lovely girl, who reminded us all of the character in 'Rising Damp' the TV series. You know, the woman who lived in Rigsby's house and appeared to be a little bit prim, but incredibly warm hearted and kind. I think it is fair to say that Sue changed her attitude completely towards life when she discovered the joys of sex! She and Pete had an almost insatiable appetite for each other!

I was so impressed with the fact that they didn't really emerge from Pete's room, so soon after they'd met each other, for nearly two weeks! It was quite common for Andy and I to bring them their meals to their bedroom! It was almost like the 'Love in' that John Lennon had with Yoko Ono, when they stayed in bed, in front of the TV cameras, for a very prolonged period of time.

I think I was secretly quite envious of the antics that were going on. I remember cruelly setting up some posters all around the hostel, describing the new sporting event at the current Winter Olympics called the 'Sexual Section'. On my poster I listed the main competitors from the United Kingdom as being Sue and Pete and described the nature of this event in detail! I vividly remember all the inmates of the hostel queuing for our evening meal and studying one of my posters, and wondering what I was going on about.

Despite this, Sue and Pete were my great friends during all of our medical school years. They had a reputation for doing outrageous things, such as not turning up for the examinations when they felt that they had not done enough swotting! This was a very brave thing to do in those days, because it was quite easy to be expelled from the medical school for not appearing at the exam hall.

Other very important players in my life at the Moullin Memorial Hostel include colourful characters such as Paul Overton, who was a very lanky, John Cleese type of character, studying electrical engineering at Imperial College. His main claim to fame was an incredibly irritating habit of walking into my room, regardless of what I was doing and helping himself to whatever beverage I might be drinking. This might have been a cup of tea or coffee or even a beer or Coca Cola.

Regardless of what it was, he would always come in, purse his lips and take a sip. I got so fed up with this after about six weeks into my medical school training that I remember urinating into an empty can of Coca Cola and leaving it on my desk waiting for him to come in. The inevitable happened, as he strolled through the doorway greeting me with the usual "Hi Mike, how are things going?" He picked up the can and took a deep swig. "Ooh," he said, "that's filthy! What is it Michael?" I looked at him intently and said, "Piss, Paul, piss!" He stopped doing it after that, which was quite refreshing.

Other notable and lovable characters at the hostel included people like 'Rodge the Dodge' a slightly overweight and very cheerful chap with, again, the long 70s' hair, a taste for Players No 6 cigarettes and cider. More interestingly perhaps, he had a marked curiosity for women from the Orient. It wasn't long before 'Rodge the Dodge' had attracted the charms of a tiny (in fact miniscule) Japanese student who was over here learning English. In contrast to his rather portly bulk, she truly looked minute and it wasn't long before they were engaged to be married.

I always used to 'bum' cigarettes off 'Rodge the Dodge' but we had a very strict deal and I had to give him five pence per fag. This, of course, was an awful lot more than the market price, but at 10.30 down the dark corridor on Sunday night, I wasn't really in much of a position to barter for any better deals. Roger was always up late and would even let me have his last cigarette, if the price was right.

Rodge also had an interest in motorcycles and of course with this mutual interest, we were both quite close to all the other lads in the hostel, who used to store their motorbikes in a small shed outside the kitchen area, on the right side of the house. That shed area still exists and I can see in my mind's eye the line-up of at least five motorcycles, all in various states of disrepair, belonging to that small group of enthusiasts who loved our hobby so much. Roger in particular was always repairing his BSA single and there was a variety of oily parts in his room on most days of the week. Even I got bitten by the bug to rebuild a motorcycle engine.

Caught in a Flap!

One of my most vivid memories was starting a complete rebuild of a Yamaha 125 twin two-stroke motor on a Friday night and working on it throughout the weekend. The engine was precariously placed on my desk and all my medical student books had been pushed aside to make space.

By Sunday evening, around eight pm, I put the last screw into the engine case and sat back to light up one of Rodge the Dodge's No 6 cigarettes. I opened a can of Harp Lager and congratulated myself on such a brilliant achievement.

On glancing down at the floor, I saw a small black ring made of rubber lying by my chair leg. I picked it up to inspect it and to my absolute dismay, realised this was one of the crank case oil seals that had been omitted from my marathon engine rebuild! I felt as sick as a parrot. I had spent the whole weekend rebuilding the engine and now I would have to go back to square one and start all over again! Looking back, I don't know what made me do this, but I decided there and then that I would start the whole job from scratch. As dawn approached the following morning, I remember slumping into bed in a state of absolute exhaustion and having one more No 6 fag as I admired my handy-work sitting on the desk.

The engine was complete and if I remember correctly, running beautifully, but I was too knackered to start my new student attachment at the hospital, working for an eminent paediatrician. I would pay for this serious omission of duty by being firmly castigated by this senior consultant the following day, when he insisted that I saw him in his office, to explain why I had not turned up for my first day on his firm. The only thing that saved me was the fact that Dr Frolick was a fellow 'petrol head' with a penchant for exotic Lancia sports cars. When I told him the truth about what I had been doing on the Sunday night, I was curiously let off any serious punishment and in fact ended up some years later being one of his last senior house officers!

The Moullin hostel offered a wealth of enjoyable experience for young people who had just left home for the first time. I cannot really remember ever working hard enough to justify my status as a medical student. Everything seemed to be left to the very last minute and in particular the preparation for the exams. Life at medical school generally was quite hard and if only

Caught in a Flap!

I'd known how difficult it was going to be to tackle the examinations, I'm sure that I would have been far more conscientious during my early days in the Moullin hostel.

I should really have followed the examples of other proper swots like John 'Donkey Dick'. John was a marvellous chap, who literally lived in his room and only came out for meals. He was in the medical school year above us and was incredibly conscientious and extraordinarily knowledgeable about his craft. Whenever there was anything I didn't understand in my studies, I would simply walk five doors down the corridor, knock and he'd always say "Come in", in his broad Geordie accent. He was always helpful and used to relish explaining the things I didn't understand. No matter which subject we were studying, John always knew the answer, but he seemed to command an extraordinarily strong understanding of the subject of anatomy.

To this day, I still can't believe that the University of London expected us to learn Gray's anatomy at the same level of detail as being able to recall the entire 'A to Z of London', without omitting a single street or direction. The only thing I can think of that comes close to this task is what London cab drivers have to do when they take the 'knowledge'. At least their job is a little bit easier because they just have to know the names, roads and directions, without having to explain what everyone does when they get there! Despite John's marvellous faculty to explain everything, there are still things in anatomy that I don't understand, despite having read them thousands of times over.

I still don't know what the 'lesser sack' of the stomach really means, or for that matter what the 'greater sack' of the stomach really is! I remember trying to learn the cranial nerves and work out which one does what. I found that I was only able to remember them on a short-term basis for about half an hour, so I'd have to swot all this in the hour leading up to the exam and hope for the best. An hour after my anatomy exams finished, nearly everything that I had learned before had simply evaporated from my brain.

This was all in stark contrast to 'Donkey Dick', who had the most amazing encyclopaedic knowledge of everything that was going on and still to this day, when

I see him 35 years down the line, he can remember much of what he learnt.

For such a quiet reclusive sort of chap, it was peculiar that all of us in the hostel seemed to cotton on to his enormous dimensions. I think many of us thought that he was wasting his very large member, because he was so quiet and committed to his studying. 'Donkey Dick' will always remain as one of the big enigmas of our Moullin Hostel days. In other words, a well endowed, pleasant, affable chap, living in a hostel full of ballet dancers and yet seeming to take very little interest in any of them!

There were lots of other people at the Moullin hostel, which I would be happy to describe in detail, but time and space will not allow for this. The community there was remarkably stable and new arrivals weren't that common. As a result, I developed a very deep friendship with many of the inmates. We used to revel in playing practical jokes on each other and because everything was so self-contained within the building, we didn't really have to go anywhere else for our entertainment, although we did have a pub around the corner. We could make up our own parties in the evening by using the large lounge area or even the marvellous attic well up in the rafters, where there was a games room with a huge snooker table.

My 21st birthday was in that room and we turned the snooker table into a bar area. Everyone danced the night away, happily banging our heads on the low rafters, as we got more and more drunk. The hostel was run by wardens and a variety of them were there during my five-year stay. The one I remember most vividly was Mrs Martin, as she had an unfortunate habit of knocking on the bedroom door, just at the crucial coital moment!

We weren't allowed to have girls in our room after 11.00 pm and Mrs Martin was really good at doing patrol duty at about 11.15 to 11.30pm. When you heard those ominous three slow knocks on the door, you realised that all subsequent activity of the sexual nature should contain itself immediately, before one got into serious trouble or even worse, expelled from the hostel! I just wonder how much virginity was protected by Mrs Martin's judicious use of her night patrols.

Caught in a Flap!

One evening when Helen was in my room (and still to this day I can't remember why she was there); I heard a knock on the door and remembered that I'd already had two warnings about this sort of behaviour. I frantically asked Helen to climb out of the window and held her by the arms. I then said "Come in", after the ominous third knock.

All Mrs Martin could see was my bum at the edge of the windowsill and my torso hanging out of the window. "What are you doing, Michael?" she said. I said, "I'm having a cigarette", I answered, "and Debbie doesn't like the smell of the smoke in my room." "OK", she said. I was frantically hanging on to Helen's wrists, as she was sliding further and further down the wall. I remember trying to pull her up, only to find that both of her perfect breasts had got stuck underneath the outside window ledge!

It was quite a problem getting her back in and at one point I was tempted to let her go because I knew the balcony below wasn't too far. She finally got back in, bruised and a little the worse for wear. I believe her ballet class the next day wasn't very comfortable, particularly during the boob-bouncing high jump dance steps!

There were also tender, but hilarious moments at the hostel. Across the corridor from me was a very nice girl called Katrina and her boyfriend had my name. Mike, worked in the television business, as part of a lighting crew and Katrina was a student at the University of London doing languages, if I recall correctly. Katrina was a cuddly girl with an ample bosom and a really generous, kind and warm personality. She had lovely rosy cheeks and reddish bobbed hair. When you looked at her you always felt happy and cheerful, because she had such a nice friendly welcoming face.

One night I particularly recall (because I was studying on this rare occasion) was spent in my room. All of a sudden I heard a particularly loud fruity cough coming from Katrina's room. The cough became more persistent and louder as the evening progressed and I noticed that she hadn't been down for dinner that evening. I knocked on her door and a very feeble voice said, "Come in". I entered and saw Katrina looking somewhat pitiful in her bed, covered in perspiration, with bright red nostrils and dark rings under her eyes. She looked really ill.

"Katrina," I said, "You look dreadful". She said, "I feel dreadful, Mike." I asked if she'd eaten anything that day." She said, "No, I've been in bed for the last two days and Mike's been away on a studio trip." It transpired that Katrina hadn't eaten anything decent for the last 48 hours and had only been drinking some sips of water. I immediately went out and got her some sustenance from the local Kentucky Fried Chicken shop.

Then, having tucked her up in bed, I offered to stay the night in her room, because she was so ill. Would you believe that Katrina said to me, "Michael, are you really trying it on with somebody as ill as I am? Can't you see how awful I look? I'm practically dead!" I said, "Don't be ridiculous I'm just trying to help."

To this day, I'm not sure whether Katrina believed that I was a 'finger-licking-good closet necrophyliac' or not, but she did let me sleep on the floor to guard her that night!

The level of practical joking going on at the Moullin hostel had no boundaries as far as I was concerned. One of the funniest things that the lads ever did, when all the girls had gone off to play a football match, was to bring the newly-introduced 'cling film' food packaging into the female lavatories. We were able to cover all the toilet bowls with a perfect coating of this cellophane, which was not visible from any angle. Even with the lights on, one could not see the reflection in the transparent film. For some reason, the girls had been on quite a long journey and were all dying for a wee when they got off the mini bus. We lads were sitting in the lounge watching the 'Saturday Sport' on the television.

We waited with relish to hear the subsequent screams from our frantically micturating female inmates. Apparently, all hell broke loose as at least six girls simultaneously did 'horse-size' wees over the floor in the lavatory! We couldn't keep a straight face and they soon found out who had committed this terrible crime against female hygiene! Of course, the girls got their own back in a far more subtle way. This was to be executed over the next few days or weeks when we were least expecting it.

Caught in a Flap!

I had the spark plug leads on my motorbike swapped over so, although it would fire, it would never run properly and it took me nearly a month to work out why it wouldn't. Rodge the Dodge had his tyres deflated while most of us had our beds 'apple-pied' on a regular basis, making it quite difficult to settle into bed after a heavy session down at the Wheat Sheaf.

However I think the most memorable practical joke that ever took place in that lovely Moullin Memorial Hostel environment, was when Nazi-Steve told us about the Exchange and Mart magazine selling a small listening device (bug), which could be concealed quite easily in an empty cigarette packet. This device had a microphone and a nine volt battery and would transmit a signal to an ordinary transistor radio set up at the right frequency. It was just too good to be true! Andy had a turbulent relationship with the beautiful redhead Helen. They were going through a bit of a stormy patch anyway and Helen was becoming more and more tetchy and irritable with him. We all thought that she was on the verge of making a move; even planning to leave the hostel and going to live in a flat. Andy was still very keen on her at that time.

For some unknown reason, Andy kept all of his empty cigarette packets on the top shelf of his book case in his tiny cell. His room was just down the corridor from mine and the doors were never locked, as I've already described. One night I went into his room, when he was studying in the library and detected a cigarette packet that was pointing in a very favourable direction towards his bed. I installed the battery and the bug, having made a small hole in the edge of the cigarette packet to expose the microphone. I positioned the packet amongst the others, so no one would ever notice what was going on. I turned the device on as we all retreated, waiting for Andy to arrive.

Rodge the Dodge, Paul Overton, the funny dustbin chap, I and others from medical school, who were coming over for a drink, all congregated in the local pub with our small transistor radio. What happened afterwards can only be described as absolutely hilarious. Andy and Helen were having a discussion after dinner in Andy's room and Helen was curious about the arrival of a camp bed that Andy had installed next to his own.

Caught in a Flap!

"What's that camp bed for?" asked Helen, "I haven't seen it before." Andy turned round and said, "I just bought it to make things a bit more comfortable."

Helen then asked, "Are you thinking of getting a new girlfriend or something seeing as I'm thinking of leaving the hostel quite soon?"

"No, no, Helen", he said, "no of course not, I'm thinking about getting it for . . . something else."

"What do you mean by something else?" she asked.

"Well, I thought I might get some company when you've gone," said Andy.

"That's exactly what I mean," said Helen, "you're thinking of getting another woman."

"No, no Helen, I was thinking about getting a pet", he said

"A pet!" exclaimed Helen, "a pet in a camp bed? What on earth do you mean by 'a pet'?"

"Well, I was thinking about getting something like . . . uhm . . . . Well something like an 'amster or an Alsatian or something."

We all nearly died laughing in the pub, huddled around our tiny transistor radio, as it gave out this crystal clear immortal 'one liner' about a camp bed and a hamster! We thought this was the funniest thing we'd ever heard and we all rushed back to the hostel to share the news with the other lads in the lounge. As we approached the lounge, the radio was still on and the conversation was still going between Helen and Andy. At this point things were getting a little bit more amicable and Helen was obviously accepting the offer of the camp bed that night.

There was a rustling noise on the radio followed by Andy saying. "Helen."

"What is it now, Andrew? I'm just agreeing to stay and keep you company this evening."

"Helen, can I ask you something?"

"What is it?" she said, rather irritated.

CAUGHT IN A FLAP!

"Helen, you've got a lovely botty."

"What?" she said.

He continued, "Do you mind if I feel you're botty?"

At this point we all erupted into laughter again. What a romantic line. "You've got a lovely botty and can I feel it." We were hysterical, but unfortunately we were very close to his room and he said, "That's funny Helen, it sounds like someone's listening to us." And we all started to laugh again.

"What do you mean someone's listening to us?" asked Helen. "Well, I said you've got a lovely botty and I'd love to feel it and someone started laughing", answered Andy. At which point we all cracked up again.

He said, "That's really strange Helen, I am sure that people are laughing downstairs."

By this time, we were crying with laughter down in the lounge but we did manage to contain ourselves. We shut up immediately, in the hope that Andy would carry on his sexual activities. It all went quiet in his room, then we heard some more rustling and Helen said, "OK then Andrew, you can feel my bottom, but you'd better be quick." With that we all erupted and Andrew's botty-feeling experiences came to an abrupt halt, as he suddenly realised that he was a victim straight out of a scene from the film 'MASH'.

I used to get into quite a lot of trouble at the hostel and one of the big things that I got into 'deep shit' for, was due to the fact that I was too lazy to get out of bed at night and go for a slash like normal people! The rooms were tiny, the corridor was long and the boy's bathroom was quite a long way down on the third floor. One night, I got fed up with going out in the cold, having had my usual skinful of four pints of Fuller's ESB, that I thought, why don't I just pee into a wine bottle instead?

I looked into my bedroom cupboard and there was an empty wine bottle. I filled it up without any difficulty whatsoever and put it back into the cupboard. The next night the same thing happened and seeing as I had drunk a bottle of wine that night there was another empty bottle so that I could also fill that one and put it into the cupboard. On Sunday night, the same thing

Caught in a Flap!

happened again and as luck would have it, I had been drinking another bottle of wine with Debbie and I was able to use that one as well. Unfortunately, I was starting to lose track of how many bottles of wee there were in my cupboard.

Anyway, to cut a long story short, after about six weeks of this intermittent wine-bottle-filling activity, the cleaning lady, Beryl, had come into my room one Monday afternoon and unfortunately she'd opened my cupboard door and discovered that some of my heavier garments in the form of a motorcycle jacket and leather trousers, had fallen off the hanger and knocked over three out of the 18 bottles of putrid, stale, stagnant urine.

My whole room was awash with rancid pee, the smell of which was staggering and poor Beryl was absolutely shocked. She tearfully ran downstairs to tell the warden that she'd come across a huge stash of Mikey's urine.

That night, I arrived home and was summoned into the warden's office. "Michael, something very serious has happened in your room today", she said.

"What was that, Mrs Holland?" I asked.

"Beryl has knocked over gallons of urine stored in old wine bottles in your cupboard. Would you like to explain why they were there?" inquired Mrs Holland.

As quick as lightning I thought of a marvellous excuse.

"Mrs Holland, I've been doing a physiological experiment on urine production in young adolescent males, in relation to alcohol intake." "Oh," she said, "a physiological experiment. What are you hoping to find out?"

I took a deep breath and said, "I believe that when a male is intoxicated, he pees out more than he drinks, leading to a state of dehydration".

"What did you find with your experiment?" she asked.

"I pee out one and a half times more than I drink," I said.

"Well I hope that's useful for the benefit of mankind and in the meantime, here's a mop and some disinfectant. Don't do it again!"

I left the warden's office with a huge sigh of relief and since then I've stopped peeing in wine bottles at night.

I have mentioned some of the tender moments in the Moullin Memorial Hostel, but there are also some quite sad ones. I remember quite a touching story about a very pretty girl called Carol who was a successful ballet dancer. She had come back one evening in a terrible state, realising that as she had been caught on the underground without having a valid ticket she was now in big trouble with the police.

Carol came in through the back door of the hostel with her mascara dripping down her red cheeks. "What's the matter sweetie," I said, having known her for quite a few years and being one of her best friends. "Mikey," she said, "I'm in terrible trouble. I have been stopped on the underground without a ticket and I'm going to have to go to court and I can't bear to tell my mummy and daddy." "Carol, do you want me to do it for you?"

I said consoling her with my arm over her lovely shoulders. "Yes please," she said.

She gave me her parent's phone number, so I waited for the appropriate time to ring and went into the little scruffy phone booth at the end of the corridor on the ground floor. "Hello, Mr Ryman," I said. "Good evening. Who's speaking?" he answered. "It's Mikey, a friend of your daughter Carol," I said.

"Yes, why are you ringing and not her?" he asked.

"I've got some bad news," I said.

"Goodness," he said and then went very quiet.

I said, "I'm afraid Carol's in trouble."

"You filthy little swine! What have you been doing to my daughter? How pregnant is she? When is she due? Why didn't you take any precautions? Why are you being so irresponsible? How do you have the nerve to ring me up and tell me now?" he quizzed, getting completely hysterical with his everlasting questions.

Then I heard him screaming for his wife. "Anna, Anna, Carol's up the duff and this little prick on the phone is trying to explain it to me." I said, "Excuse me! Excuse me; I'm only trying to tell you that Carol was caught on the underground train without having a valid ticket." There was a stunned silence.

"Oh God, what a relief," he said, "what a relief. Please tell her we love her very much and we can't wait to see her again. Good bye."

I went up to see Carol. She looked forlorn and very agitated in her small room, hiding under a duvet cover with a comfort blanket.

"Mikey, what did mummy and daddy say?" she said nervously, with tears rolling down her mascara-stained face.

I told her, "They said they love you very much and can't wait to see you again".

"Don't be ridiculous", she said, "Tell me the truth."

I said, "I am telling the truth" and I left her room feeling quite smug with the marvellous hug and delicious kiss that I had been rewarded with! To this day, I'm not sure whether Carol ever found out the true content of my conversation with her parents, but the bottom line is I don't think she got into too much trouble.

Chapter 6
Nazi-Steve and the tactical crap

It's funny how people get nicknames, isn't it. At medical school one of the first people I met was my great friend Steve. He was colourful right from the very beginning. He'd already decided to join the army, so that he could get a decent income to support himself. He was very athletic and indulged in a wide variety of sporting activities.

He seemed to have a talent for anything. Even in the later years of medical school, he was able to build a radio-controlled helicopter, as his first venture into the world of aeronautical modelling. Helicopters are the most difficult things to fly and most people start with simple gliders. Steve built this during his house job at Windsor and was able to control it beautifully. I still find this most embarrassing because even now at the age of fifty plus, I can't even fly a basic electric aeroplane without difficulty.

Because Steve was in the Army and he had blond hair and blue eyes, my mother naturally christened him Nazi-Steve, even though he was from Wales. It is strange that this name has stuck ever since, as far as our entire family is concerned. Steve was always very cheeky to my mother as a result of the name that she'd bestowed upon him. In return, he used to ring her regularly on New Year's Day usually a few minutes after midnight and greet her with a resounding, "Happy New Year, Sue, how are your tits?" Mum never seemed to take offence to this and even when Steve was approaching his mid forties, the greeting would still make its way to my mum on a regular basis.

Steve's main forté was in organising things and on this occasion he took an active part in arranging our famous boys' week together, as fourth year medical students, when we took a barge down the Avon River sometime in a chilly March. Looking back, this was a mad thing to do, bearing in mind that we were in the middle of our pathology block, which was probably one of the most difficult parts of the course. We really should have been swotting. Pathology, at best, is a dreadful dreary subject and the pathology block was an intensive series of lectures going on for many weeks, all centred on very boring pictures of tissue seen under the microscope. If this wasn't bad enough, the terminology used in pathology was almost like memorising a foreign language.

Anyway, we decided to take our 'boys-on-tour' trip right in the middle of this exceptionally important part of our education and you can guess the rest of the story; I failed pathology! The members of the crew included Steve Chimebells, who can only be described as a tall, softly-spoken philosopher type of chap who seemed to put an awful lot of thought into everything he said and did. He always seemed to be extraordinarily realistic and 'matter of fact' about everything in life. That's not to say he hadn't got a marvellous sense of humour, it's just that he organised his life in such a way that it never seemed to have any blips or blemishes. Even when he was planning his family, many years later, he discussed the issue in great detail with me, so as to enhance the level of organisational control.

He was the only bloke I knew who had the nerve to 'shack up' with a woman much older than him and end up practically rebuilding her house, not to mention doing her plumbing, central heating and electrical work, all whilst he was a student! He seemed to be away for months at a time, but nevertheless always managed to turn up for the exams and, needless to say, passed them all.

This adventure started when I drove my ancient blue Volkswagen Beetle down to somewhere on the River Avon with the most enormous barrel of real ale perched precariously on the back seat. It was a cold damp afternoon and I vividly remember the mist rising from the water on the marina. Steve and I lugged this huge barrel of beer out of the car and down onto a very spindly-looking little pontoon. Our barge was waiting a few yards further down the pontoon and I remember feeling quite impressed by its size. It was one of those old steel canal barges, with a marvellous chugging marine diesel engine in the back and tiller steering.

The accommodation looked quite splendid really, with approximately five large births, a full kitchen galley unit and a nice lounge area. We were quite thrilled about the prospect of our boys'—own holiday.

However, that was soon going to change. My girlfriend at that time was the tall slim ballet dancer called Debbie.

Caught in a Flap!

She was very keen to come on this holiday with us insisting that a woman's touch would be essential on a 'boys'-own' trip, particularly seeing as we would need someone to cook and look after us. This did not make much of an impression on Nazi-Steve, who was quite adamant that this should be a boys' trip but Paul Sydney, our other intrepid explorer and Steve Chimebells didn't seem to be too put out by the suggestion. Obviously, I was under a considerable amount of pressure and at the end of the day, the vote went in favour of Debbie coming along with us.

This trip will go down in my memory for two main reasons. First of all it introduced me to the concept of the 'tactical crap', courtesy of our good friend Nazi-Steve. Secondly, it confirmed in my mind the relative importance of women in a world ruled by bachelors.

We set off on our famous barge trip on that cold misty morning. I remember wondering why we had chosen such a miserable time of the year to go. The reason was simple. It was cheap! Shortly after setting off, it became obvious there was a question about the toilet facilities as we realised there was only a limited amount of storage for human waste within the confines of our particular barge. We, therefore, all made a democratic decision that we would only pee in the lavatory and try, if it all possible, to open our bowels on shore rather than on the boat!

I think the initiative for this move mainly came from Debbie, as she was frightened of the prospect of a terrible pong originating from four medical students, whose basic diet was going to be real ale, lamb Madras, pilau rice and garlic nan bread, (not to mention sag aloo and tarka dall) for the next seven days!

We reluctantly agreed to the notion of not being able to 'dump' on the boat and Nazi-Steve of course, was the first to suggest a military solution to our new problem. He put forward the idea of a 'tactical crap'. He said that this was something he'd learned in the army during his training. The idea was that you were able to open your bowels in such a position that you could still see what was happening with regard to the enemy.

It was quite a difficult manoeuvre, which supposedly involved pulling your trousers and underpants down around your ankles and placing yourself in a position supported by your legs and your arms, in such a fashion that you were still able to more or less sit up and look around. This, of course, was not the same as sitting up directly in a squatting position, because the enemy would be able to see you. In fact, it was almost like being on all fours, except of course your back was facing the ground and your tummy was facing the sky.

We could not wait to see this manoeuvre in action so we decided to find a quiet part of the river and moor up to witness Nazi-Steve's demonstration of his trick. He got off the boat quite near the bank and found a suitable spot asking one of us to look out, by standing on top of the barge and making sure that there were no other people in the adjacent fields and hedgerows.

We assured him that everything was all right so he got himself into position, pulled down his trousers and underpants and prepared to demonstrate. Obviously, he would need a toilet roll thrown to him at the crucial time. Just as he was ready we noticed a young family of hikers approaching quite close to where he was. We did the honourable thing and told him the coast was clear. Just as he started to perform, the family was within close proximity to the action. Naturally we cast off the barge and took the toilet roll with us!

I can remember looking over the stern at this rather frantic figure caught in full view of a family of five, whilst in the throes of a large bowel movement, with no prospect of any toilet paper or, indeed, a transport facility to get him out of this terrible situation.

Nazi-Steve sulked a bit after that!

Chapter 7
Hooray For Henrietta!

At a recent reunion to celebrate my 51st birthday (my 50th birthday was a damp squib as I'd cancelled it because there was so much trouble going on at the hospital), I had the company of my three best friends from medical school. Nazi-Steve, Steve Chimebells and Paul Sydney had all turned up to join me for a nice weekend at our cottage.

Before we went out to see the annual Guy Fawkes' firework display on the heath, followed by dinner at our favourite restaurant in the village, we enjoyed some pre-dinner drinks by the fire. It was a clear, cold November evening, just perfect for reminiscing by a fireside. One of the topics of conversation that came up was the story of Henrietta who was a medical student in our year and I think it's fair to say that she made a measurable impression on every single hot-blooded male at the medical school, including us. She was a statuesque blonde, who was incredibly good looking. She had a lovely figure, with what appeared to be a gravity-defying bust line and most importantly of all, she was charming, refined and beautifully brought up.

To make her even more interesting, there was a slight naivety about her, as she sometimes didn't grasp some vulgar humour in rather common jokes. 'Periods' weren't called menstruation; they were called the 'curse'. We hate to think what terminology she used to describe sexual intercourse! The icing on the cake was that she came from a very rich family and even had a brand new car to drive around in when she reached 21. I remember this aquamarine blue Peugeot 104 taking us down to Brighton for a sunny Wednesday afternoon trip to the seaside.

Despite Henrietta's amazing grace, glamour and overwhelming attraction, I confess that not one of us in our little league of friends even came close to dating her, let alone going out with her on a long-term basis. However there was one young lad in our group called Ivan who was a very well turned out young gentleman and very reminiscent of Mark Phillips who was trying to attract the charms of Princess Anne at the time. He wasn't quite as posh as Mark Phillips but, nevertheless, spoke the Queen's English very well and was good at disguising his background as not being quite as affluent or middle class as Henrietta's. Ivan was not a typical 'rugger bugger', running around in a leather jacket as part of a group of six or eight 'hit men'. These hit men comprised a group of rugby players from our year who prowled around the student union building on a regular basis during our time at medical school. I can't even remember Ivan being particularly athletic.

He did, however, share my interest in fast cars and motorcycles and one of his main claims to fame, given his relatively slight frame (rather like mine), was that he could still handle a large Z900 four cylinder Kawasaki with a certain amount of skill. This impressed me enormously, as well as his other motoring aspirations later on during our careers, such his acquisition of a Triumph GT6 sports car.

For some reason, Henrietta and Ivan became an inseparable pair during those early years at medical school. They used to sit in the lecture theatre together, eat together and walk around the medical school together. In fact, Steve Chimebells, Nazi-Steve, Paul Sydney and I became so envious of this relationship that we nicknamed Ivan 'Ivanoma'. The inference of being an 'oma' was that he was like a tumour joined on to Henrietta. Wherever Henrietta went her tumour was there with her. We got this idea after going to a lecture theatre and hearing a pathology lecture about tumours growing on legs.

One of these tumours was called a sarcoma and we imagined that if Ivan could choose to which part of Henrietta's body he would like to be permanently joined, it would probably be in the vicinity of her legs! The name 'Ivanoma' stuck all the way through medical school, as he followed her around through the full five years of their training. Even when we were allocated to smaller student groups to do our clinical work, Ivanoma and Henrietta were inseparable, always appearing together on the ward rounds and being 'on take' and 'on call' together.

To this day, we don't know how far their relationship actually progressed, in terms of intimate contact and so forth. They probably just remained really good friends and mutual companions during those often difficult years at medical school. One thing is for sure, the rest of us were jealous. Curiously, Ivan never showed any evidence of jealousy, even when it was abundantly obvious that some of the medical staff were taking a great interest in his companion, Henrietta.

We all remember vividly, the SHO in general surgery, who presented himself on the professorial ward round as a strapping hunk of a guy and looked as if he could annihilate our 1st 15 rugby team in one fell swoop. Not only was he good looking and well built, but he was also the Prof's SHO. Judging by the body language between him and Henrietta and vice versa, we all became acutely aware of the possibility that Henrietta was interested.

I cannot ever recall Ivanoma showing any signs of remorse about this situation. His friendship with Henrietta continued unabated. Even when Henrietta arrived late for a ward round having had a lunchtime date with the strapping senior house officer, Ivan appeared completely unmoved by the spectacle, despite the fact that we were all fuming!

Throughout our training the fascination with Henrietta never subsided. She always remained intriguingly unobtainable, but in the back of our minds I'm sure we all felt that there might just be a minute chance of getting lucky with her. This feeling of optimism, however, was rapidly blown out of the water one cold February afternoon over at the West Middlesex Hospital surgical unit. Nazi—Steve, Paul Sydney, Steve and my good self were all attached to the same 'firm' as Henrietta, Ivan and Kathy in the urology surgical department. This lovely old hospital, with its ancient Victorian outbuildings, played a very important part in our training.

It gave us a real opportunity to do hands on work and deal with real patients, simply because it was very busy and there was so much experience available. Unlike working in a big teaching hospital, there were opportunities to take one's initiative and carry out tests and investigations on patients. This was provided one had the blessing of the SHO involved with that firm. We really did get involved with our patients and followed them through all their management pathways.

I can remember one elderly gentleman, who was waiting to be investigated for the possibility of leaking urine through his back passage. All this sounded very peculiar to me, because there didn't seem to be any definite pathology to account for this peculiar presentation. On the evening before surgery, when I went to see him and to talk about his operation, I noted that he already had a catheter inserted into his bladder. On thinking about this further, it suddenly crossed my mind to put some blue ink into his catheter to see where it came out. I asked the house officer if it would be all right to do a 'catheter and dye' study and she gave me permission. I put the blue dye in and waited for half an hour, then went back and did a rectal examination.

On inserting my finger into his bottom, I found the blue dye was coming out. I had made the diagnosis of a rectovesical fistula. I felt very clever with myself and was eager to present my findings on the consultant ward round the next day.

The next day arrived and I waited impatiently for my turn to present my case. It was the end of a rather long preoperative ward round but, nevertheless, I was able to describe my findings. I went on to proudly present my train of thought to the consultant, in front of, the lovely Henrietta. Later, after lunch, we all prepared to go to theatre to see our patients being operated on. As it was a urology list, there was a lot of cystoscopy being done. Steve, Nazi Steve, Paul Sydney and I walked into theatre, just as they were preparing the first gentleman for his cystoscopy.

His legs were up in stirrups and what struck us and literally took our breath away, were the enormous size of his genitals. He had a pair of testicles the size of hot cross buns and it is safe to say that his penis resembled a large rolling pin, hanging down leisurely between his two enormous testicles.

I gulped in amazement and exclaimed in a very screechy voice; "Christ chaps, just look at the size of that warhead!" We all drew breath simultaneously and gazed in astonishment at the size of these monstrous genitals. At that point the theatre doors reopened and there was the radiant Henrietta standing in some exquisitely tight blue theatre gear.

We all waited to see her response. She glanced casually over to where our patient was suspended in the lithotomy position with all his family jewels on display. Henrietta took a long look, followed by a slow sigh and then uttered the most unforgettable sentence we had ever heard.

Caught in a Flap!

"Ha," she said, "couldn't do much with that".

She then serenely walked out of the theatre, leaving us all in a state of stunned silence. Any aspirations that any of us had, about exposing any of our private parts to Henrietta, at any point in the future, were rapidly and irreversibly extinguished!

Chapter 8
The Story Of The Burning Buttocks

During my life there have been some highs and there have been some lows. Some of the lows have been so desperately awful that, at the time, I did not believe that things could get any worse than they already were. I loved living at the Moullin Memorial Hostel and the news that I had to leave was devastating. My mum organised my transfer from my cosy little room in that marvellous building stuffed with beautiful ballet dancers.

This was on the grounds that she thought I was being distracted from my medical studies by a certain ballet dancer of tall stature. I found myself packed and ready to go to the dreariest, most dreadful hostel in Muswell Hill, which was full of religious fanatics. So awful was this place that I've actually forgotten its name but I remember arriving at this gloomy building with dark corridors and low ceilings. It was reminiscent of a crummy motorway hotel, frequented by door-to-door salesmen and reps with boring company cars.

Caught in a Flap!

The worst thing about this place was the dreadful public address system which would not even allow you to have a quiet afternoon nap without breaking your slumbers by a screeching voice coming out of a loudspeaker saying, "Telephone call for room three, telephone call for room three!" In fact there was no escape from this and to make matters worse, there was a rota to do the telephone duty so that you, yourself, could screech out these terrible messages to all the other inmates. Life at medical school had to continue and the trip from Muswell Hill to the hospital wasn't easy.

I used to leave my motorcycle at Muswell Hill station and take the dreaded tube all the way down to Hammersmith. On one particular weekend when I was a medical student on call, something quite extraordinary happened.

For some strange reason, I found myself on a continuous tour of duty, which kicked off on Friday evening and finished sometime around Sunday lunchtime. I thought this was unusual, because most medical students' shifts were usually for one night. I'm not sure why I got so embroiled on this shift but it was probably to do with the fact that the SHO I was shadowing was truly gorgeous and probably a very good teacher as well. Sarah Dominion was the girl in question and she was teaching us surgery.

She was vivacious with orangey red hair and a lovely beaming smile, as well as a totally bubbly personality. I'm sure that this was the reason why I stayed in the hospital, wearing the same set of theatre clothes for nearly three days! The on-take was particularly hectic and there were lots of admissions coming in with plenty of work for eager shadow medical students. It was so busy and the patients were spread out so thinly over such a big hospital that we found ourselves constantly going from one ward to another, usually climbing the stairs of the 15 storey building, rather than using the lift.

Very little sleep was had during that time, because things were so frantic and I cannot actually remember going to the on-call room for a rest. What I can remember is that after two days of constantly walking around in the same set of theatre clothes, the area between my buttocks was starting to chafe and burn. I was getting what was known in medical circles as on-call gluteal chafing, more commonly known as 'arse burn'.

Caught in a Flap!

This was aggravated by not changing clothes, staying in the same pair of underpants and more importantly, not having a wash. By the time Sunday afternoon arrived, I was walking around the hospital holding my buttocks apart with my hands to stop them rubbing together. The pain was excruciating and my walk down to the tube station, through the cemetery, must have looked comical to any passers by. Sitting on the tube seat was total agony and I couldn't wait to get back to the dreary hostel, just to have a shower or a bath. At that time, I knew nobody there and had no one to speak to, so I felt it was quite appropriate to have a wash, followed by a good rest in front of the television.

I retired to my gloomy room with its window facing out towards the girls building across the road. After my bath, I found it very difficult to dry my bottom because it was so sore and I had a huge blister on each cheek. I flung myself onto my tiny student bed, flopped my legs and liberally spread Vaseline all over the inflamed area around my bottom. As I glanced up between my knees contemplating my war wounds, I saw the most sickening sight. Three of the girls across the road were looking at me, through their bay window, with binoculars. I nearly died! What could be going through their minds, what with the sight of a male lying in a vulnerable position covering his entire bottom with Vaseline?

I didn't know what to do, because if I'd jumped up and ran to the window it would only make the situation worse. If I buried myself under the blankets, the curtains would still be open so I cut my losses, rolled onto the floor and crawled over to the window to pull the curtains across, hopefully without the girls seeing any more of my exposed torso.

To this day I don't know who those girls were. I had unconsciously blanked out what their faces looked like, in an effort to shield my embarrassment when I arrived in the dining room later on for tea. It will come as no surprise to the reader that I acquired the nickname of 'Vaseline alley', by some of the less charitable Christians in that dreadful institution.

Chapter 9
The Grand Slam

I think it is safe to say that, given my disastrous performance as a medical student, I was truly blessed when it came to house jobs after qualifying. I have so many fond and hilarious memories of being a student, but it is fair to say that I was a lazy sod who hardly did any work. I spent most of my five years really enjoying myself in the Moullin Memorial Hostel, along with all those lovely ballet dancers.

Surprisingly, the only examinations I passed first time were the finals. In those days, one had the opportunity of sitting two sets of examinations to procure a place as a qualified doctor. The first and obvious option was to continue with the university you were attending and take their degree at the end of five years. In London, this was called the MBBS. You also had the opportunity of taking the Royal College examinations, which were called the Conjoint. The Conjoint gave you extra letters in the form of MRCS and LRCP. The joy of taking these college exams early was that you could actually qualify before the other students in your year, who were taking the university examination.

I decided that after a desperately awful career at medical school, I would try to redeem myself by passing both the Conjoint and the final MB examinations at the same time! It is difficult to imagine how any of us got through this double examination, which was called the 'Grand Slam'. If it wasn't bad enough taking finals just once, just imagine what it was like doing everything in duplicate. In my case, it was even worse, because I had just failed the pathology exam the year before (which needed re-sitting) and it would therefore be added to the repertoire for my final examination performance!

In a nutshell, I basically found myself doing examinations continuously for a period of no less than six weeks. This really was tantamount to torture. Constant revision, constant worrying and constant sleepless nights (particularly the night before one of the big examinations), all led to a rather miserable existence.

At that time I was living in student accommodation, courtesy of the University of London. This was because I had escaped from the dreaded 'God Squad' hostel. The initial weeks of gloom and despondency at the university accommodation (which comprised a converted 1920s hotel), were soon superseded by the joys and revelations of realising that I was one of the most senior student residents living there. This made me fair game for the attention of the young preclinical girls, who were also residing there. One in particular was lovely. She made me Sunday lunch nearly every weekend and more or less adored me.

In return, I used to help her with her preclinical studies and impress her with my fortitude, in the face of the overwhelming task of trying to sit two major qualifying degrees at the same time! This girl was so nice, that she even used to treat my dad to Sunday lunches on his rare visits over from the West Indies, to see me in London. The sad thing is, I've already forgotten her name, but I do remember what she looked like, with her slight frame, brown bobbed haircut and piercing blue eyes. She was really nice to me and I think she made a major contribution to my forthcoming success in the examinations.

Eventually, the dreadful six weeks were up and I'd completed all the examinations in both examination centres. Those at the university were quite familiar, as the environment was simply where I had been working on the wards for the previous three years. However, the college examinations were not familiar and took place in quite a formidable environment. These large conjoint examination halls had really dark basements, with garish lime green paint everywhere.

The hard wooden benches, down in these basements, were occupied by nervous looking students frantically doing last minute revision. The lavatories were crammed with unfortunate individuals, suffering from erratic, unpredictable and sometimes explosive bowel movements, secondary to their overwhelming nervousness!

I'll never forget those days of the examinations, as being spent in such unwelcoming surroundings. Here we were, in our smart two or three-piece suits, presenting ourselves in front of the examiners in a state of almost abject terror. The unpredictability of the whole situation made it worse. Would I get a simple straightforward patient with diabetes, who would answer all my questions, or would I get some complete nutter with Alzheimer's disease, giving me a complete run around the houses with his Munchausen's syndrome?

You could never predict what you were going to get. The feeling of relief when you sat down with a patient who looked sensible and immediately started to answer your questions in a helpful and cooperative way was actually quite overwhelming. Anyway, I won't bore you with the details of all my clinical examinations which continued over those long six weeks, but I will describe what happened at the medical school bar at the end of my ordeal.

It was a Friday afternoon and I walked into the bar only to be greeted by the huge frame of Glyn Keloid. Glyn was a great big Manchurian lad, who played rugby and had marvellous aspirations of becoming a famous surgeon. His overwhelming confidence and anatomical knowledge at our dissecting table had more or less bewildered and demoralised us over the years. His overall belief in his own self-worth and ability made us all feel quite inferior.

We knew that Glyn was going to be a great surgeon and thought perhaps we might be lucky enough to become GPs. Over the years, in particular during the clinical part of our training, Glyn was always able to make me, especially, feel as if I wasn't going to make it. Having started my life as a disastrous anatomy student, who never knew anything, Glyn had come to terms with the fact that perhaps I might know a little bit about breasts and bottoms, but very little else.

I found it extraordinarily difficult to remember even simple lists of names. For example, when faced with the overwhelming task of trying to describe where the vagus nerve actually went in the body, I think that I would have had more luck in memorising a telephone directory!

In fact I was so bad at anatomy, that in one of the viva oral examinations, I got scored the lowest mark possible! This was a 'gamma' as opposed to an 'alpha' or 'beta'. Within minutes of this revelation, the whole year at medical school was nicknaming me 'Gamma-James'. Well, I suppose this made a change from 'Scrotum Scalp'! Anatomy wasn't the only examination I struggled with and I think it's fair to say, that I had probably more than one go at nearly everything during my training.

This was particularly embarrassing for my poor dad, given that he was a Professor of Physiology at the University of the West Indies. In my second preclinical year when I failed physiology, I think my mum and dad were sitting in a dark room somewhere in Jamaica, with the curtains drawn, drinking gin and tonic and commiserating with each other.

Nevertheless, finals had come and gone and now I was in the bar greeting Glyn. He walked up to me and offered his commiserations, "Oh don't worry lad, it'll be better next time." Intrigued by his comment, I suddenly seized the opportunity that I for years had been waiting for.

"Glyn", I said, "didn't you just go down in conjoint surgery this afternoon?"

"You're right, a bit of bad luck," he said, "but I was able to pass my MBBS, so that means at least I'm qualified."

Des Parunia

I looked at him and took a long, deep breath and started to relish the words that I was about to utter.

"Glyn, today I passed Conjoint and the MBBS. You know, the 'Grand Slam'. I think it should be me saying to you 'better luck next time'. Would you like to buy me a pint?"

Needless to say, he didn't.

Later on that afternoon, the joy of my clever response to Dr Keloid was wiped out, by a sarcastic quip from one of my fellow students. As I was walking down to the tube station I bumped into a Navy-sponsored student called Des. After qualifying, bearded Des wanted to be a medic on a submarine. He was on his way to his last examination and had already heard the news of my own good fortune.

"Good luck this afternoon Des," I said amicably.

His sarcastic reply surprised me.

"Well Mikey, if you can pass these flaming finals then I guess anyone can." I pondered on his reply and realised that not all doctors are kind and thoughtful people, including myself! "I hope you drown you bastard," I muttered quietly under my breath, as we parted company.

After my monumental success in the finals, I suddenly became incredibly inflated and thrilled with myself. This situation was exacerbated by finding myself in a professorial house job after qualifying. I managed to do this, even though I took a long break after my finals, messing about on a motorcycle in the south of France. My first house job was working for the Professor of Medicine and this was a singularly thrilling experience for me, because the professor used to be a good friend of my dad's when he worked in London.

I think this may have made up for my failing physiology three years before! I had a lovely room in the hospital accommodation and was genuinely thrilled with the camaraderie and friendship that I had with my fellow junior colleagues. The biggest bonus, of course, was working with all those lovely student nurses.

It is true to say that even with the 'one-in-two rotas' where you worked everyday, every other night and every other weekend, life was undeniably great because of all the fun that we had together. I was lucky enough to move on to my second pre-registration house job and this time I was working for the Professor of Surgery. This is where my story of the big man begins.

Chapter 10
Tall Men Walk Quietly

I truly loved working for the Professor of Surgery. I thought he was fabulously famous and the most important surgical textbook of our generation was edited by his good self. Every time my bleep went off I would say "Professorial Surgical House Officer speaking". I must have sounded so arrogant and irritating to many of my colleagues. The whole idea of being on the professorial surgical team was thrilling for me. Not only was the surgery exciting, but also there was this lovely feeling of prestige and kudos associated with working for such an eminently famous person and somebody that everyone knew.

I remember dad hearing my news of achieving a second professorial house officer position at my home teaching hospital. I still have his letter written from the West Indies where he was a Professor himself, saying that he didn't know anybody who had achieved two professorial house jobs in their own teaching hospital. I think it was completely inappropriate for me to be so puffed up and thrilled with myself, given my very mediocre background, from the point of view of examinations 'success'!

Nevertheless, at the end of the day I was doing my second pre-registration house officer job in another professorial department. Even my close friends such as 'Germs', found the whole thing quite amazing. Jeremy's background, with his dad being an eminent surgeon at a very prestigious teaching hospital, reflected an attitude that he just really couldn't understand why someone like 'Gamma James' could have got two such high profile jobs. To this day I don't really know why I deserved those positions, but the memories associated with them are still fresh and very funny.

There is something very nice about having a feeling of self worth and thinking that, even for a transient time, you might be something special or just a little bit more important than the average doctor!

The irony is that all it takes is one astute colleague to put you right back in your place by bursting your ego-bubble in one fell swoop! The individual concerned was another marvellous surgeon called Mr Peters, who was an extremely accomplished urological surgeon with a special area of expertise in 'sex-change' operations. I admired him for many reasons, but probably the most important of all was his splendid hobby.

I have always been a 'petrol head' ever since I can remember, having developed a strong fascination with the internal combustion engine and an insatiable appetite for trying anything new or different that involved motorcycles or motorcars. Even as a young medical student I was fortunate enough, on my 21st birthday, to relishingly spend the £400 present from my mother and father on the most immaculate second—hand Yamaha. This particular model was a RD 350 two-stroke sports motorcycle.

It was a dead-ringer of the motorcycles that I had admired as a spotty teenager living in Rhodesia, because the British South African police force used the very same machine as the workhorse for all their patrol work in that lovely country. The thrill of getting this bike on my birthday still remains and I get goose pimples when I remember picking the machine up in Richmond, at a private address, sometime round three o'clock on a gloomy winter afternoon. I relish the memory of pulling out onto Richmond High Road and watching the front wheel lift up, as I effortlessly changed from first to second gear without even having to slip the clutch! What a 'wheelie' that was!

At that time, I really thought that I had 'arrived' in the world of motorcycling. Isn't it strange that this 39 horsepower wondrous motorcycle should now pale into insignificance when I think of what I use today on a regular basis? My current hack, a 200 mph Suzuki Hayabusa 1300 GXR can accelerate to 60 mph in about two and a half seconds and can probably do more in second gear than my little Yamaha did flat out! Once again I digress!

Mr Peters was a fellow 'petrol head'. He was a senior consultant at several teaching hospitals, but found that his passion was for Alfa Romeo sports cars. The thing that really impressed me the most was that he had an Alfa Romeo Spider. Anybody who has seen the film 'The Graduate' with Dustin Hoffman and Anne Bancroft will remember the bright red Alfa Spider Duetto that Dustin Hoffman drove across America to rescue his lover from being married to the wrong bloke. I had seen the film when I was about 13, on a family trip to America to stay with my parents' best friends. I remember always wanting an Alfa Spider Duetto.

As a medical student I was attached to Mr Peters' firm. I remember his marvellous banter in theatre with the nurses. Everybody was frightened of him because he was so strict and precise. His ward rounds were so tightly organised and brilliantly orchestrated that it really was mandatory to practise rehearsing your patients' case presentations on the night before the Monday morning round. It was quite common, as medical students, for us to go in on a Sunday night just to check our patients and rehearse our histories and presentations just to make sure that everything was perfect for Mr Peters' ward round.

Mr Peters was so particular about patient care that he would be extremely angry even if only slight misdemeanours were spotted. He would absolutely hate it if a patient's catheter had not been strapped securely to the leg of that patient, in case there was a possibility that a loose catheter could be tugged or pulled on inappropriately and cause the patient unnecessary discomfort. He was particular about the way his dressings were applied to the surgical wounds and more importantly how frequently they should be changed.

I think it is fair to say that every student nurse on the urology firm found themselves in fear and trepidation of Mr Peters' ward-round. I had an intense admiration for him based on his incredibly dry sense of humour. He did gender reassignment operations and I often found myself in theatre with him in the middle of an amputation of the male organ, leading to the subsequent refashioning of the pelvis to create a new vagina.

These operations used to make me feel very queasy. It all came to a head one day when, just as I thought I was getting used to the penile amputation and subsequent refashioning and construction of a vagina using the scrotal skin . . . . he quietly chopped off this chap's member and tossed it over his shoulder! He then said quietly to the sister, "Here you are, give it to the cat!" At that point I felt myself becoming very light headed and on the verge of passing out. As there are a lot of cats about, I find it very difficult to forget this story!!

That was not all. One of my most vivid memories is of him stripping the penis of its skin prior to amputation and noticing that the patient was starting to develop an erection! Mr Peters then curtly retorted to the anaesthetist saying, "Come on Jack, give him some more anaesthesia he's starting to enjoy himself." At that point, I also remember having this overwhelming desire to pass out.

Anyway let's get back to Mr Peters' marvellous hobby. Not only did he own an Alfa Romeo Spider Duetto just like the one in 'The Graduate', but also he did something quite extraordinary with it. I believe, although I've never had full confirmation of this fact, that when he took delivery of this beautiful Italian two—door soft top motorcar, he took it back to his residence where he had an ample garage.

He then completely dismantled the vehicle and rebuilt it the way he thought it should be built! At that time, in the mid-to-late seventies, Alfa Romeo had a terrible reputation for build quality and poor quality materials, particularly the mild steel that they used on the chassis and body work. Rumour had it that Mr Peters would completely rebuild his car, re-underseal it, regalvanise it and then put it back together the way he though it should be made.

I thought this was an amazing engineering task for such an extremely busy and talented surgeon. I followed his example in buying an Alfa Romeo Spider at the first opportunity I ever had sometime in 1991 when I was a registrar in Ascot. That is another story altogether which I will return to in due course.

Going back to Professor Hardon-Brains and the thrill and excitement I had working with him, I have so many memories of all the things that were happening at that time. First of all, the Professor was coming up to his retirement and I believe I was his last ever house officer. He taught me so much in such a short period of time and the amazing thing is that I've retained so much of his advice and knowledge. It is true to say that I hung on to every word he said. Possibly this is because everybody around me was so much in awe of him and he just seemed to be a rather larger-than—life character.

I often think about those post-war 'Carry on Doctor' and 'Doctor in the House' films. There was one character in particular, called Sir Lancelot Spratt, who was the great chief surgeon at the hospital. Those films showed Sir Lancelot Spratt as being larger-than-life and everyone hanging onto every word that he said. I thought that 'Professor' was another Sir Lancelot Spratt.

One of my favourite memories of being a medical student before I had even qualified was attending his outpatient clinic on a cold Thursday afternoon. He had asked me to take a history and do a cursory examination on a new patient. I was then required to present it to him and the other students attending the clinic.

I remember the gentleman very well. He was enormously overweight, smoked 30 cigarettes a day and had difficulty with the circulation in his legs. He was unemployed, had very few teeth left and drank an enormous amount of alcohol on a daily basis. He was supported by social services and had 8 children because of a complete lack of regard for any kind of contraception.

Half of his children were playing truant from school and the other half were on social benefit as well because, like their father, they were reluctant to go out to work. I took a history of this patient's claudication (in other words, the pain that he was experiencing in his legs on exertion). I was also able to allude to the fact that he had so many children, was not at work and very reluctant to go back to work because of his condition. The professor asked me to present my case and I did so as best I could.

Then he said in front of all the medical students in the room, of which there were about eight, "What are your thoughts about this patient?" My reply was, "Well professor, I think he has quite a lot of difficulty with his circulatory system in relation to his habitus and his lifestyle." The professor said: "No, I mean what is 'your' impression about this patient?"

"I'm not sure I understand what you mean, Sir", I said.

"Well", he said looking at me over his spectacles; "I would say that this patient is an absolute slob! He has clearly got nothing going for him and makes absolutely no effort to either help himself or those around him. Now he comes along with clogged arteries, self-inflicted after years of alcohol abuse and excessive cigarette smoking, expecting to be cured! Unfortunately it is our job to sort him out."

What a refreshing attitude, I thought. This man is just so human and so sensitive, not only of the needs of patients, but also of the educational needs of naive and impressionable young doctors in training. Professor's observations of human beings, as well as life in general, will always stay with me as an example of a novel and stimulating way to teach. I will never forget him.

So let us return to the original story of the tall man. I haven't mentioned that the professor stood at well over six feet and was impeccably dressed, therefore fulfilling the marvellous role of the Sir Lancelot Spratt character from those fantastic vintage comedy films. He used to call his junior house officers 'dressers' just like the Victorian surgeons used to. A dresser in those days was somebody who literally dressed the wounds after surgery.

They were apprentices in surgery, rather like the junior house officers of today. I loved operating with the professor, being called 'dresser' and being allowed to put the stitches into the skin after he left. I enjoyed putting on the bandages afterwards. I loved the whole traditional atmosphere of his preoperative and postoperative ward rounds and the fact that everybody knew exactly what their job was and more importantly, where their place was.

Having said all that I could not resist the temptation of exploiting the fact that I was working for the Professor in the last few months leading up to his retirement. As he was getting closer to that date, when he would literally finally throw in the towel and stop practising, his clinical workload was starting to diminish quite significantly. I remember the operating lists were becoming lighter and lighter in the ensuing weeks. There was one weekend in particular that I remember so vividly, because his professorial ward was virtually empty.

It was a Saturday morning and I was still doing a one-in-two rota as I have described before. This meant that I was doing one weekend on then one weekend off, as well as working every Monday to Friday and every other night! I was relishing the opportunity of a quiet weekend because, if there were only a few patients on the ward, it was less likely for me to be called or interrupted during my indulgences in that marvellous nursing home. I was also looking forward to the other frivolous activities that were going on within the environs of our grand new teaching hospital. The venues for these activities included the hospital social club, the curry house across the road, the Italian restaurant, the Greek kebab house, and of course the endless number of parties and get-togethers going on in a multitude of rooms in those three tower blocks crammed with junior doctors, student nurses and qualified nurses!

On this particular weekend, I arrived on the ward to do the routine postoperative ward round. As the professor was winding down, we had only done two very simple cases that required overnight admission and the other patients had already been discharged after day surgery. The two cases in question were a young nurse who had had a sebaceous cyst removed from under her arm and another woman who'd had had a straight forward haemorrhoidectomy.

The rest of the ward was virtually empty apart from a few long-stayers from other consultants. I remember having a slight hangover from the night before following a rather good party in one of the nurse's rooms. I greeted a rather lovely young staff nurse who was in charge of the ward that Saturday morning. No sister had been in place because of the light workload anticipated over the weekend.

I just couldn't resist it, having realised how few patients there were on the ward and I said to her. "Bryony, I know this is the professorial unit and I know that Prof is on his way out with the prospect of imminent retirement. I also know that we've only got two postoperative cases. The first one is a 'Mickey Mouse' sebaceous cyst under the arm, which, I'm sure will go home in the next few hours and the other one has got a sore bum with her haemorrhoids.

I doubt that this will require any of my expert attention. For that reason, please, would you be kind enough to keep the number of bleeps to a minimum and let me try to recoup some of my energy, so that I can carry on enjoying this rather quiet weekend during the last throws of the professor's departure. In other words", I finished cheekily, "Bryony, please try not to let either of these crushingly boring cases disturb my enjoyment over the next 48 hours." Bryony looked at me motionless. At that point there was a little tap on my left shoulder. I turned round rather quickly to see six foot plus of towering professor standing behind me which made me gulp!

"James", he said in a slightly sarcastic lilt, "don't you know that tall men walk quietly and little men make a lot of noise!" I can still remember the student nurse behind the drugs cupboard on the nursing station, doubled up in muffled hysterics at that moment when my professorial bubble was truly burst!

Chapter 11
The Story Off The Exploding Toilet

One of my most memorable stories as a young house officer at a teaching hospital in London involved the inevitable in-between girlfriends scenario. I had just split up with Debbie, the ballet dancer from the Moullin Hostel and found myself, as a newly-qualified young doctor, living in the hospital digs. I had no fixed abode, as I was doing locums at the time and mainly spent most of my life sleeping in other people's rooms in the doctor and nurse accommodation. My best friend Steve Chimebells was a full-time house officer and he very kindly let me use his floor in the lounge to sleep on, which was on the 14th floor of one of the residences.

Those were very exciting times because I had no fixed home, no fixed job and was completely footloose and fancy free. I earned my living at that time doing locums in a variety of hospitals and really enjoyed the complete freedom of not having to work for more than a few weeks at a time. However, I did need a girlfriend and there just happened to be another Debbie on the scene. This one was a beautiful young thing of about 19 years of age. My friend Matthew, who came over from Rhodesia to visit me shortly after we qualified, had spotted her momentarily before I had. Needless to say it was Matthew's good looks and suave personality, not to mention his marvellous African suntan and accent that won her hands down over me!

However, Matthew did need to return back to Rhodesia. I made it my duty to 'look after' Debbie while he was away. It wasn't long before I realised that my role as caretaker needed to be upgraded to the role of boyfriend!

Debbie was quite heavy going as far as conquests go, because you never really understood where you were with her. Did she fancy me? Did she just like me as a friend? Was she just quite keen to continue a platonic relationship? Or was she just aching to fall in love with me? I did not know, but nevertheless I asked her for a date.

A few short evenings in the local pub, perhaps punctuated with the odd sessions of live music down in one of the more interesting locals, made up the beginnings of our relationship. Still in the early stages, she did invite me to her flat in the nursing home for dinner one evening. Debbie was on the 9th floor and shared a lovely flat with several other girls. One girl in particular called Gail was another stunner with thick dark hair and unblemished white skin.

On the evening in question, I found myself inexplicably nervous. I had terrible wind that had been troubling me all day. In fact it is fair to say that I basically had uncontrollable flatus, which wasn't only frequent but extraordinarily noisy. Nevertheless, I prepared myself for my date and did the usual things (as we said in Rhodesia) of having 'a shit, shower and shave' before going out! I presented myself appropriately ablutioned and nicely turned out. However, the terrible wind was still there. Debbie invited me into her cosy little room. She was wearing one of those full length caftan dresses from the 60's and her appearance was very reminiscent of one of the girls on the front of the 'Woodstock' album cover. She reminded me of the beautiful actress Kathryn Ross from 'The Graduate'

It was no good, despite polite conversation the wind was frantically building up in my lower gastrointestinal

Caught in a Flap!

tract. I did the courteous thing and excused myself to go the lavatory, which was in the corridor of the girls' flat. There were four rooms altogether in the flat and they were all very close to the very flimsily built, mutually shared convenience. I closed the paper-thin door behind me and decided what the best strategy would be to do an enormously loud fart without attracting undue attention. My first plan was to cough very loudly and let rip at the same time. I started coughing frantically, and then stopped.

This was immediately followed by an enormously loud thunder crack of a fart!! I felt completely demolished that my plan had failed. I then decided to blow my nose loudly and blow off at the same time. I grabbed the tissue paper, started blowing my nose and then just as I stopped, I blew off catastrophically loudly!! At this point I didn't know what to do because I was sure the two girls in the flat could hear what I was doing.

I then decided, in desperation, to pull the toilet chain and then blow off while that was happening. I pulled the chain, flushed the toilet and didn't quite keep up with the situation. I did a crackerjack of a fart at the end of the flush which nearly blew the door off! By this point

I did not know where to turn to next. I couldn't think of anything else to do apart from cut my losses and just leave, but then again I had been looking forward to seeing Debbie all day. I did the honourable thing. I walked into Debbie's room and said, "I'm really sorry I took so long but I couldn't get into the lavatory Debs because one of your flatmates was in there and it sounds like she's got a terrible tummy upset." "Gosh' said Debbie, 'I didn't realise that Gail was so ill". "Anyway" I said, "I hope Gail gets better".

Debbie and I continued to have a very lovely evening and I left not too late, given the decorum that was expected on a first date. As I was leaving however, I bumped into Gail in the corridor and very discretely pointed out that I was going early because Debbie wasn't very well with a terrible tummy upset. I had to do this to cover myself as I was absolutely certain that Gail had been hearing all the exploding noises during the course of the evening.

The next morning Debbie and Gail met in the kitchen for breakfast. Gail politely asked Debbie whether her tummy had recovered. Debbie looked at Gail in total amazement because she thought it was her with the tummy upset. The pair of them looked at each other and must have realised what had happened.

Fortunately, I had left the scene of the crime at least 12 hours before. I still wonder whether they realised it was me or whether each thought that the other had a genuine tummy upset and was really trying to cover it up.

As I never raised the subject again with either of them, I don't think I will ever find out.

Chapter 12
The Story Of Mr Reynolds' Bag

My own teaching hospital offered a marvellous opportunity for me, as a junior house doctor, to simply have endless fun. I have already mentioned the tower block nursing home as well as a similar tower block doctors' residence overlooking the River Thames. The social club was always a delight, being within crawling distance of our residences and having two bars. There was one upstairs and, one downstairs as well as full sport facilities and a lovely Olympic-size swimming pool.

At the end of every evening ward round in the main hospital building there would be a flurry of white-coated young doctors, making their way down the escalator into the main entrance hall and out into the front promenade of the hospital towards the social club. The evening ward round would also mark the time when the girls on nightshift would be taking over and releasing their counterparts, who would naturally all be quite thirsty and looking forward to a quick pint in the pub before going home.

The hospital club was therefore full of student nurses, regular nurses, medical students, and regular junior doctors. I can vividly remember the appearance of the upstairs bar overlooking the swimming pool, where the entire wall from one end of the building to the other had little coat hangers covered with white coats and stethoscopes draping out of the big pockets.

This special evening time was truly precious to us all, as it usually marked the end of a rather long day and the beginning of a rather interesting evening! Throughout the 15 floors of the two nursing homes and the doctors' residence there would be literally hundreds of parties going on. These would range from small gatherings of two or three people making a spaghetti Bolognese, to much larger affairs with copious quantities of alcohol and lots of dancing. You could never be lonely, as a junior doctor, as there was always a lovely young nurse to talk to in the hospital club after work and almost invariably an invitation to go back and have coffee or join in one of the parties or supper clubs.

There was obviously always a downside to these activities. One of the most memorable ones would be the concept of being caught on duty with a few too many onboard! It was easily tempting to get carried away at these parties and forget that you had the bleep for the medical or surgical on-take team, or even worse the cardiac arrest bleep. I tended to curtail my drinking activities when I was on-take, but when I was just doing the ordinary on-calls for the wards then that was a different story altogether!

I can remember clearly the evening when I was the ENT house officer for the wards and there were only a handful of inpatients, including the odd child recovering from a tonsillectomy. The adult side of the ENT was very rarely busy, but it did have a facility to take on the emergency admissions from casualty. The commonest ENT admission from casualty, out of hours, was invariably the inevitable nose bleed.

This was known as epistaxis. On this particular occasion, I had been in one of the nursing home rooms enjoying a really good party with some of the girls from the geriatric ward. This was a particularly happy crew of nurses working on that unit at the time. Most of them were students and I remember we had just piled into Carol's flat after our usual few drinks at the hospital club, at the end of the shift.

We had all been drinking 'Snake Bites' for most of the evening and some of us were certainly a little worse for wear. I remember approaching Carol's flat, as we all tried to work out which pizza house we would be invading that evening to get our late night supper. As I went to the front door of the flat the bleep went off and I got a call from the staff nurse on the 10th floor where the ENT ward was. I tried to answer my pager as efficiently and professionally as possible, but I do remember I was already starting to slur my words.

In the background, the staff nurse must have heard all the outrageous giggling going on, as this gaggle of girls tried piling into the flat near where I was making my telephone call. I was summoned to the ENT ward to see a young gentleman, who had presented with quite a heavy nosebleed. I duly obliged and made my way over to the hospital. On arriving in the ENT treatment room, I pulled up my tie and made sure that my hair looked neat, while I frantically sucked on an Extra Strong Mint. I introduced myself to the sister-in—charge and proceeded into the treatment room, where there was a young man wearing denims and a check shirt. He had quite a significant nosebleed, which he was trying to control by pinching his nostrils.

Accompanying him was a rather anxious-looking girlfriend, who was quite smart wearing a tweed skirt, a beige polo neck top, and a little pearl necklace around this. She had a bob haircut, lace tights and rather smart shoes and she looked like one of those more upmarket girls, probably training as a solicitor or something like that. I introduced myself to this couple and then duly explained that I was going to have a look up the affected nostril and gently pack the nasal cavity with a gauze ribbon, soaked in a cocktail of lignocaine and adrenaline, to relieve the pain as well as the bleeding.

Sister Jeanette arrived with the appropriate stainless steel tray, the Tillie's forceps and the appropriate amount of ribbon gauze. I put my little ENT headlamp, on so that I could see what I was doing and just before I was going to start, the young woman enquired about how much blood her partner had already lost. "Do you know how much blood he's lost already, given that he started bleeding like this about an hour ago?" I looked at her quizzically and with all the intellect that I could muster for this monstrously hard question I replied. "No more than you would do in an average menstrual cycle, my dear."

At this point the sister shot me a devastating glare and I stopped this conversation immediately. I proceeded to pick up the ribbon gauze with these delicate nasal forceps and asked the gentleman to put his head back in the reclining seat, so that I could look up his nostrils.

At this point I was aware of the peculiar sensation of seeing four nostrils rather than two. I suddenly realized that the alcoholic double vision was kicking in. I started packing the nostril with the long thin ribbon gauze. To my amazement, it appeared that the blood loss was still continuing, despite my efforts. At this point the sister politely pointed out that I was packing the wrong nostril.

She very gently guided me out of the treatment room and into the nursing station. "Look Mike", she said, "I think we should call your friend Steve Chimebells. Let's call it a day and let you go to bed, eh?" "Yes, Jeanette", I said politely, leaving the ward. But poor

Steve Chimebells was interrupted yet again during one of his nights off to come and bail me out. I retreated back to the party letting switchboard know that my best friend would be covering me for the foreseeable future.

The next morning I found myself in Mr Reynolds' operating theatre. Mr Reynolds was a fantastic general surgeon with an international reputation for biliary surgery. He was an amazing character whom we all admired. He used to love smoking and always joined us medical students in the medical student union bar after work for a pint and a fag. As he perused his admiring entourage he made fantastic diagnoses on us, such as spotting a discrete swelling in the neck of one of the rugger buggers.

"You better come and see me tomorrow young man. I think there is something wrong with your neck," he would say and he was always right. His operating theatre was an experience in itself. Halfway through difficult cases he would leave the table and lie down on the theatre floor and light up. More often than not the cigar break would go on for 15 to 20 minutes, while he contemplated the next part of his difficult surgical campaign on the patient who was lying next to him, albeit on a higher level!

On the particular morning in question, when I was in theatre with Mr Reynolds, there was a very pretty student nurse in theatre who was quite clearly overwhelmed with what was going on in there. We were in the middle of a seven-hour liver operation and Mr Reynolds was well into his stride. I couldn't resist it. I looked at the little nurse and said, "I think you'd better empty Mr Reynolds' bag." Her piercing bright blue eyes glanced towards me and she said, "What bag are you talking about, Dr James?" I said, "Well, for these cases Mr Reynolds wears a 'Peniflow' catheter system which allows him to relieve himself during the extremely long operation."

The student nurse was clearly conversant with the 'Peniflow', because she had been doing the geriatric rotation and looking after loads of incontinent men who were using these devices. She also knew that the 'Peniflow' ran down to a bag that was usually attached to the calf muscle of the man wearing it.

She very obligingly got down on her knees and started working her way underneath the drapes of the operating table where Mr Reynolds was standing. She had started palpating up his leg at which point he suddenly exclaimed, "Nursey, what are you doing." She replied instantly, "I'm looking for your bag, Sir." "Good God", he said, "It's much higher up than that!" Needless to say that student nurse never ever talked to me again.

Later on that afternoon Mr Reynolds excelled himself again, by walking into the anaesthetic room where his next patient was lying, looking peacefully anaesthetised. This patient was down for a rhinophyoma reduction operation. This was intended to remove a huge great protuberant swelling on his nose. "Christ!" said Mr Reynolds, "just look at the size of that geezer's conk!"

The anaesthetist looked immediately alarmed and I looked quizzical, until the point where the old man lifted up his eyelid and said, "Come on Mr Reynolds, it's not that bad." It's funny how un-anaesthetised patients always have the irritating habit of answering back.

Caught in a Flap!

I got through the rest of the day in theatre without too much in the way of untoward events or calamities. I started to contemplate at around five o'clock, what my night off would bring me. I was safe in the knowledge that I wouldn't need to see any epistaxis patients with four nostril holes. My fervour was instantly diluted, however, the minute I got back to the flat and Steve Chimebells reminded me that I owed him a night after he'd covered me the night before!

Well, I thought, there's always the social club at handover time.

In this day and age, the junior doctor's club is a pitiful sight with a few sad lonely individuals having a drink on their own. The junior doctors no longer live in and they don't do the usual on-call nights anymore. The shift system has taken over, the nurses have all gone and there is nobody left. Those lovely memories of the pretty student nurses in their little blue 'Jay Cloth' dresses and lovely starched white hats will remain with me forever and so will the memory of Mr Reynolds' non existent bag!

Chapter 13
A Typical Day In The Life Of A Gynaecology SHO

I have chosen a particular day that remains firmly engrained in my brain for a number of reasons. First of all, it is my only living memory of ever waking up in the morning with a truly filthy hangover brought about by over indulgence in neat Scotch whiskey. I don't know how I ended up going round to see a very attractive blonde staff nurse called Cass, who was looking after her friend's house while she was on holiday.

They called it house-sitting and I'm sure the term still applies today. Cass was a very lovely paediatric staff nurse, whom I'd met during my attachment as a paediatric house officer working for the very eminent Dr Frolick. I had remained friends with Cass after moving on to gynaecology and on this particular occasion she invited me over to her friend's house to have a drink and perhaps a light supper.

CAUGHT IN A FLAP!

All I can remember about the evening is getting there quite early on my silver Honda CBX motorcycle. The house was somewhere near Twickenham and if I recall it wasn't very far away from the hospital. My girlfriend Debbie was doing night duty as a student nurse at the time and was obviously not going to miss me on this occasion! I arrived to meet Cass on my motorcycle at about 7:30pm.

I remember being very impressed by the comfortable, semi-detached three bedroom house that she was looking after. Within moments of my arrival we were both sitting on the settee drinking Bells Scotch whiskey. To this day I'm not sure where that bottle came from, though I certainly don't remember bringing it with me. In any event, it appeared and we started drinking rather large measures of this potent amber-coloured liquid over the next two to three hours. I remember feeling completely drunk at about 11 o'clock and being very politely invited to stay the night, because I was in no condition to ride my motorcycle home.

I vaguely remember lying on a double bed in a pair of 'tightening' white underpants, with Cass lying seductively next to me in just a white T-shirt and matching knickers! It is quite extraordinary that no form of sexual activity took place and I recall that we simply had a very long conversation while we lay on this bed before passing out. In the morning I woke up with what can only be described as a 'mother of all hangovers'. To make matters worse I had the prospect of a gynaecology operating list during which I was expected to assist my esteemed boss Mr Collins.

I knew I was going to be late as soon as my bloodshot eyeballs were exposed to the bright morning sunshine creeping through the curtains. I remember that my tongue was truly glued to the roof my mouth, which felt like the proverbial bird cage. I staggered into the bathroom and brushed my teeth, washed my face and got on my bike. The ride to my digs on that big Honda 'six' can only be described as precarious as I wobbled through the rush hour traffic.

God knows how I didn't get arrested, or fall off, or both! I frantically arrived at the flats and rushed up to the 15th floor to get changed and ready for work. I then rushed into the front entrance of the hospital and made my way to theatres on the top floor. I then got undressed and hastily put on my theatre greens and proceeded to theatre, hopefully arriving there before my boss put in an appearance.

Needless to say, I was desperately late and Mr Collins had already started the first case with the registrar Mr Brown. I walked into theatre to offer my grovelling apologies at which point Mr Collins in his usual clipped gentlemanly-type manner said, "For God's sake, get him out of here, he's a fire hazard!" The boss was obviously referring to the dreadful alcoholic fumes coming out of my body, secondary to that lovely evening of binge drinking and Scotch Whiskey with the lovely pert-breasted Cass.

As usual during that particular period of my life, the day didn't really get much better afterwards. I returned to theatre a few hours later to find Mr Brown doing a laparoscopic sterilisation. Mr Brown had just put the sharp pointed skewer like object, called a trocar, into this woman's abdomen through her umbilicus. He had already filled her tummy with gas so that the abdomen was distended and ready to be skewered. As he pulled the sharp trocar out we all gasped in amazement to see there was a big brown blob of faeces on the end of the skewer. "Hm", said Mr Brown, looking through his stylish hippie type glasses. "I wonder what that is."

As he said it, the bristles of his moustache seemed to be twitching rather nervously. "Well", said the sister, "if you don't know what that is then I think you're in the wrong specialty." We all realised that Mr Brown had hit 'the brown', the brown stuff that is! Mr Brown sniffed the trocar and then made the decision to open the women's abdomen and repair her large bowel. Needless to say, that in my post—intoxicated state, I wasn't a particularly masterful assistant and Mr Brown expressed the appropriate degree of irritation all the way through this unplanned procedure!

Later on that afternoon I found myself in the gynaecology clinic with one of the most popular consultants in the hospital. The clinic was wretched for me, because each time I picked up a set of notes and asked the patient to come into my consulting room they said they didn't want to see me. They wanted to see Mr Pullsome. Mr P was a real smoothy with a lovely soothing voice, a fantastic bedside manner and a charming personality. He really liked his patients and it wasn't unusual for him to write in the clinical notes; 'On examination, super girl. No signs of anaemia'.

I can't imagine what would happen to me today if I wrote something similar in my patient's contemporary records. All the patients adored him and they didn't want to see the senior registrar and certainly not the poxy SHO. Another downside was that his clinic would go on forever because there were so many patients he had to see. Of course we had to stay until the end of the clinic, as was the accepted form in those days. I remember feeling truly left out.

After the clinic I retired to the nursing home to meet the lovely Debbie and found myself trying to explain why I was still reeking of alcohol and more importantly, why I hadn't come home the night before!

Chapter 14
Another Hard Day At The Orifice

I can recall very few occasions as a junior doctor, where a 36-hour shift at the hospital was so punctuated with gaffs and frivolity worthy of a really gaudy old music hall pantomime. There is one however, which still makes me quietly snigger whenever I think about it.

The period in question was during a teaching hospital appointment in the early eighties and involves a variety of colourful characters. The day started as usual in the gynaecology operating theatre, where the senior registrar was doing his list. Percy Plungaire was a highly skilled and confident South African with a wicked sense of humour and a cheeky smile.

His mixed Cape Coloured background gave him amazing insight into both sides of South African culture, including the deprivation of the Townships contrasting with the white privileges of apartheid. He was therefore quite a cynical observer of human life and usually found humour in most situations he was involved in. This also included his activities in the operating theatre.

On this particular occasion, in the operating theatre, a rather plump girl from one of the posh London Teaching Hospitals had made an appointment with Mr Plungaire to discuss a job that she was applying for. Mr Plungaire was waiting to start a new consultant post overseas and Miss Pratt was keen to fill his shoes.

I greeted the rather rotund registrar and politely explained that Mr Plungaire was on his way. She asked me all about him and whether he seemed happy with the job. I described how competent and skilful he was and emphasised his marvellous teaching qualities. I reflected on the contrast between the exceedingly dull Miss Pratt and the flamboyant Mr Plungaire as I answered the questions. My life would never be the same, if she were to be appointed, I thought.

The patient was now being wheeled into theatre and placed on the operating table with her legs up in stirrups. I excused myself and prepared to wash and drape the patient. As I was completing this task, I made sure that I knew all about the case as Mr Plungaire was certain to ask. She was an attractive young woman who found it difficult to insert tampons. Furthermore she had never had a sexual relationship, having said that she would prefer to wait for marriage.

At that moment both theatre doors burst open and Mr Plungaire rushed in with a sterile glove on his right hand. "Howzit Mickey?" He asked excitedly in his strong Yarpey accent. "Is this the virgin with a tight hymen?"

"Yes . . . . but I would like to introduce you" . . . Before I could finish my sentence Mr Plungaire yelled "Geronimo!" and leapt across the operating theatre floor to plunge his examining fingers into the awaiting pelvis!

"Not anymore!" he shouted.

"Please may I introduce Miss Pratt," I said rather lamely. "She was thinking about applying for your job."

Caught in a Flap!

I remember that on the next day my boss commented on the curious fact that one of the promising female applicants had withdrawn her application for the senior registrar post.

After Mr Plungaire's list, I found myself in day surgery with yet another charismatic and suave senior registrar from New Zealand over here to complete his training. I remember that this tall, athletic, fair-haired man was good looking and could have passed as an RAF jet fighter pilot, especially when he was wearing his white Irish woollen polo neck-jersey and smoking a pipe. Peter Moore-Stiff certainly cut a fine figure of a man and that afternoon he was teaching me a new technique that he had picked up in Sydney whilst on sabbatical from Auckland.

The young patient on the table happened to be a hospital physiotherapist and was complaining of vulval irritation, associated with a disease called intra-epithelial neoplasia.

Peter had recently been trained by a famous Australian gynaecologist in the technique of using a fine laser beam to destroy the superficial top layer of skin cells and cure the itching. The theatre was full of eager junior doctors, nurses and medical students. Peter started to prep the patient and asked for some cleaning lotion to bathe the skin. I remember him liberally splashing this solution over the entire vulval area, including a luxuriant field of thick ginger pubic hair!

He positioned his laser gun at an appropriate distance from the target and lined it up to fire on the small skin lesion that he had identified on one of the inner lips. He pulled the trigger and a bright red beam of laser shot out towards the target. At that very second there was a huge sheet of flame throwing itself up from the entire mons pubis area as all the pubic hair spontaneously combusted! With immediate speed and precision, Peter grasped the first swab lying close to hand and with the help of other patting hands (including mine) doused the flames!

Sitting in a plume of blue smoke and staring at a completely bald birth canal entrance, Peter then calmly remarked in an Aussie accent "Gudday, Gudday . . . . Now that's what I call a Bush Fire!"

Caught in a Flap!

The poor student nurse who had given Peter an inflammable alcohol based skin prep solution by mistake, allegedly changed career and became a pole dancer of the bald variety, we believe.

That evening I was on call for maternity at one of West London's most trendy obstetric hospitals. At this particular time in the early eighties all kinds of celebrities were flocking to have their babies there. They were attracted by the forward thinking maternity services, which had embraced all kinds of new innovations, such as the darkness and tranquillity of giving birth in a silent gloomy room without light, or giving birth under water.

I remember reflecting on how irritated the sister on the post-natal ward was on the previous morning. She just could not believe how a certain pop star had the cheek to stay the night in his wife's bed, just after she had experienced a long and difficult labour, resulting in a particularly difficult rotational forceps delivery and a massive episiotomy! The trouble was that as soon as all the other fathers had found out about this, they all wanted to stay the night too! None of this made sense to me and I just could not understand why any bloke would want to spend the night in the maternity unit with a sticky wife, when unlimited pub access beckoned just across the road from the hospital!

Anyway, after I had done the labour ward hand over round, I popped over to see how Sister was doing with regard to the unwelcome influx of overnight male guests. Fortunately the situation had improved in the hands of a rather fierce hospital matron. Over a cup of coffee we talked about the pop star's wife. I explained to sister that I just could not understand why this tiny woman from Hong Kong would not let me inspect her bottom and check to see that her enormous episiotomy wound was healing OK.

I had been in to see her every morning for days and politely asked if I could have a look. Every time I got the same answer in a strong Honkonese accent. "No one look at my bottom," she said. "Go away!"

All I could think about was the state of her undercarriage, following that horrendous forceps delivery which required all the skill and manual dexterity that the marvellous Mr Plungaire had to offer! After all, this tiny mother had a nine pound infant extracted from her diminutive pelvis using the force from a pair of stainless steel tongs! Sister told me not to worry anymore about it, so I went back to labour ward to sew up another mother's bottom.

Much later on that night, whilst making my way back to my on call room to grab an hour's sleep, I found myself strolling across a large post-natal ward filled with exhausted mothers and noisy babies with sore heads. In the murky darkness ahead of me, I could see the silhouette of a sister walking very slowly alongside the tiny figure of a woman. As I drew closer the sister recognised me and called out softly, "Oh it is you Dr James. Would you mind having a quick look at this patient's wound?"

"Bloody Hell" I thought, "The pop star's wife has changed her bleeding mind!"

Clearly irritated with this request I replied curtly, "Oh very well then. Put her on this bed and I will have a quick look." I was buggered if I was going to accompany them both all the way back to her side room! Sister gently encouraged the tiny Chinese woman to lie down, whilst I immediately pounced and asked her to lift up her nightie. At this point I rapidly ripped off the NHS paper maternity pants the tiny mother was wearing and peered down at her bottom region using my powerful flash light. It was amazing!

There was no sign of any wound bruising or swelling anywhere near the birth canal entrance, bottom or buttocks! In fact, the stitches had been placed so precisely just below the surface of the skin that I could not see them either. "What sort of genius could have repaired this?" I thought.

I was so impressed that I that I blurted out in a 'fog horn' voice to Sister, waking up all the other mothers as I did so, "In all my experience, I have never seen such neat surgery. I cannot even see the stitches for God's sake! Sister, this is extraordinary!" Before Sister could reply, a tiny voice in a distinctly Chinese/cockney accent informed me, "But doctor . . . . I had Caesarean section last night! My bottom OK!"

That night did not get much better. In the very early hours I was rudely awoken from a brief, but very deep sleep, by the casualty officer who wanted an opinion about a young secretary who had been referred with heavy vaginal bleeding and a positive pregnancy test. I dragged myself out of bed and made my way out, through the cold night air, down towards the accident and emergency building. This department was always busy with the usual background buzz of medical activity covering nearly every specialty.

The young guy in cubicle three had fallen off his motorbike and was having his broken leg assessed by the orthopaedic registrar. The depressed spinster alcoholic in cubicle six was being treated for an overdose and the eight-month baby in the paediatric bay was being treated for projectile vomiting! "But where was my patient?" I pondered. I simply asked the student nurse on the admission desk where the young secretary was. "Cubicle nine," she said confidently.

I promptly marched off purposefully towards the cubicle knowing that if I sorted this case out quickly enough I would be back in bed in no time! I introduced myself quickly to a very attractive young woman and relying on the history given to me by the casualty officer proceeded directly to a pelvic examination. I was intrigued to find that actually she was not bleeding and her genital organs were all normal.

The student nurse chaperone was looking bemused. "Well Miss Norton, I have to say that I cannot find anything wrong down below. In fact it all looks perfect and your womb is of normal size. Are you quite sure that you may be pregnant?" "Pregnant!" she exclaimed in a surprised voice. "I only came here with a splinter in my left eye!"

"Exit stage left", I thought!

Chapter 15
Driving Home For Christmas

There is a marvellous song by Chris Rea called 'Driving Home For Christmas' and nothing evokes such strong, fond and warm memories more than hearing that song whenever it is played. As a junior doctor I did an awful lot of driving home for Christmas. What is quite remarkable about my career is, that despite doing a one in two rota (as I have previously explained) for most of my professional life, it was amazing the number of times that I was free to go home at some point during the Christmas break.

I think for the first 20 years after qualifying I had an amazing record of hardly ever having to actually be on duty on Christmas day. This was a truly remarkable record, given that in all probability I should have worked at least half of the Christmases during that time.

Looking back, I'm not really sure what motivated or drove me to behave in such an eccentric manner during the Christmas season. I seemed to have had an overwhelming desire to make the Christmas festivities as jolly and as generous as possible. This was not a 'buy Dad some socks' here, or 'give mum some cheap perfume' there, or 'treat my brothers to a new beer glass' etc. I envisaged Christmas as being a truly extravagant affair, during which time I was going to treat all the members of my immediate family and of course my girlfriend, as generously as possible. I found all of this tremendously exciting.

Even as late in my development as a junior registrar in London in the mid 1980s, I can remember being on call for the delivery suite and franticly running back to my on-call-room between deliveries. I just had to survey all the marvellous presents that I had laid out on my bed ready for wrapping, to be delivered by hand to everyone the next morning. I even extended my generosity to friends far away from me. My best friend in Africa, Phil Heath, was going to be the benefactor of the brand new James Bond digital watch that had just been brought out after a recent successful Roger Moore screening.

Caught in a Flap!

This watch had been advertised on all the TV programmes and was prominently displayed in all of the electrical shops in and around London. I had managed to find such a piece advertised in the Dixon's electrical outlet for a meagre forty nine pounds and ninety five pence. I had even found a girl to deliver the watch to my friend. She was a lovely tall dark-haired anaesthetist who was working with me as an SHO. She was about to venture on her first trip to Zimbabwe and in her luggage was Phil Heath's 007 James Bond watch ready to be delivered personally! How much more effort can you make for your best friend with a courier like that!

Just to give you an idea of the extent of my generosity, I can remember one Christmas getting ready to leave the hospital, with a rowing boat firmly strapped onto the roof of my beautiful lilac blue Daimler XJ6. I had this boat personally commissioned and rebuilt by a local boat builder at Brentford Dock. It had been restored from a living wreck of almost derelict proportions to a beautiful newly—varnished masterpiece. I had bought new oars, fenders and even a life-jacket for my dad. I knew he was about to enjoy moving down to London and living by the river, where he could pursue his childhood ambition of rowing a boat up and down the Thames.

Once the boat had been securely attached to the roof of my car, I returned to my on-call-room on Christmas eve looking at the spread of presents laying all over my bed ready for departure. I had bought my mother a beautiful mauve and violet cashmere jersey from the open-air market at Covent Garden. My brother PJ had a brand new pair of Puma soft leather trainers and my other brother Hughie had a radio-controlled Nissan 240 Z scale model car. For my lovely girlfriend Debbie, I had bought a deep purple corduroy full-length dress from Laura Ashley, which I thought she would look absolutely stunning in.

I was so excited about these Christmas trips that I didn't mind being on call for the hospital, because I knew it would probably be quite difficult to fall asleep anyway. I still relish the moment of seeing the clock showing 9 am and knowing that all I had to do was pop over to delivery suite, give a quick handover ward round to my colleague and then jump into my lovely car.

Then I would set off down the deserted motorway, in total luxurious comfort, with Chris Rea playing 'Driving Home for Christmas'.

There was also, of course, the delicious expectation of seeing my brothers, my mum and dad, the pussy cat 'Pansy Person' (a gorgeous Siamese) and little mongrel dog Lucy. That two hour journey up to Leicester was always a pleasure and I cannot remember any mishaps, breakdowns, traffic jams or anything else that would spoil a lovely Christmas Eve journey. The best part was pulling into the drive of our lovely house and going in through the front door to the loveliest warm greeting from so many people, all absolutely thrilled to see me! The smell of the roast turkey with all the trimmings used to hit me as I entered the porch, followed by the delicious waft of opened cans of real ale waiting for me and my brothers.

Christmas was almost invariably like this in Leicester, although there was one memorable mishap during that dreadful year when Debbie had decided to split up with me. What a contrast! Two days of abject misery at home trying to be jolly, after I had bought the most monumental mountain of lovely presents, for everybody in my family, including a brand new bicycle for my dad! I can recall being dropped off by my mother at a bus stop in Highgate one damp dark afternoon on my way back to the hospital. It was the end of the Christmas break and PJ was being taken back to college. I was still wretchedly depressed about Debbie and not really paying attention to anything.

I was also desperately hung over and still trying to digest an extra large portion of hot turkey curry that I had made the night before. As I stood alone in the gloom of the bus shelter, I casually let rip with an almighty explosive fog-horn fart, which nearly demolished the shelter! To my horror, I noticed in my peripheral vision, the form of a beautiful dark girl standing on a beach wearing a black bikini. "I do beg your pardon!" I shrieked, suddenly in a state of panic. I then realised that I had reached my lowest ebb, by apologising to a Jamaican Tourist Board winter holiday poster!!

All in all, the vast majority of Christmases were marvellous and the only thing that I have any regret about was that none of us seemed able to wait until Christmas morning to open our presents! I don't know when this all came about, but it was sometime in the early eighties when it became quite apparent. The Christmas present openings seemed to occur some time after midnight, just after we had finished our huge Christmas dinner. Christmas dinner in our family usually took place on Christmas Eve. None of us could wait! Having said that, it was really quite lovely, with us all gathered in the big front room by the Christmas tree. We franticly opened all our presents and then stayed up until two or three in the morning relishing their contents.

This, unfortunately, led to Christmas Day being a little bit of a damp squib from the point of view of there not being that much else to do. There is, however, one thing indelibly engrained in my mind about all of these Christmas activities. Simply, it was amazing how quickly it would all be over. One would look forward to it so much and then, two days later, it was all finished and you found yourself in a car driving back to London ready for the next labour ward shift. No matter how short the period of enjoyment was, the pleasure it gave me made it all worth while.

It's interesting to look back and think that I managed to continue this level of enthusiasm for the Christmas holidays and all the good things associated with them, right up until my early forties. It was at this point that my parents said they could no longer keep up with the pace and more particularly, they were finding it ever more increasingly difficult to find me something they could buy for Christmas that I would actually like! Since then Christmases have never really been the same.

Chapter 16
The Case Of The Mysterious Hand

Talking of Mr Plungaire's putting of fingers in unusual places, brings to mind a story about a whole hand! This memory takes me back to my training as an SHO in gynaecology in the early eighties. One of the joys of being a young senior house officer doing a one-in two rota (which is something I explained earlier), was that the hospital was obliged to give you free accommodation. Young Debbie and I had the most brilliant junior doctor flat on the 13th floor of the nursing home. The views out over London and the river estuary were stunning. My flat was particularly special as I had a rather large double bed. This was very unusual in a doctor's accommodation in those days. The hospital usually furnished you with quite a narrow bed, rather reminiscent of something out of a prison scenario.

On this particular Sunday afternoon, Debbie and I had made a splendid roast dinner and were having a quiet relax in front of the television. We watched a monumental epic called 'The Deer Hunter' which appeared to go on for hours and hours. After the film, just as we were getting ready to go out for our usual trip to the local for a couple of pints prior to our evening curry, there was a knock on the door. Paul Sydney stood at the doorway looking slightly the worse for wear. He was one of my close friends from medical school and I hadn't seen him for a few months, as he was doing a surgical job in orthopaedics at another hospital. He happened to find himself in the vicinity and knowing that I was at this hospital, decided to drop in for a chat.

Paul had a colourful career with the women and appeared to have literally dozens of girlfriends, several of which were on the go at any one time. He was an attractive guy, very reminiscent of a Leslie Phillips' character and had a very similar smooth voice. "Hello Michael", he drawled, "how are you doing my dear chap?" I said, "Paul, what a thrill to see you, do come in and have a drink". He came in, greeted Debbie with a very amorous kiss on her cheek and sat down to have a few Harp lagers with us. I was on call unfortunately so couldn't join in too much in the alcoholic festivities, but we did have a takeaway in the flat and some more drinks. As the evening progressed we were able to go over to the hospital social club and have a couple of pints of Stella Artois before adjourning back to the flat.

At this point, I noted that Paul was decidedly pissed and in no condition to drive home. I did the honourable thing and offered him the opportunity to stay in our flat and sleep on the settee. I remember he exclaimed that he couldn't possibly sleep on the settee as it would be far too uncomfortable. I gave the matter some thought and reflected on the size of our double-bed. I agreed somewhat reluctantly to let Paul sleep in the bed with me and Debbie.

We all got tucked up quite comfortably round about 11 p.m. Paul was against the wall, Debbie was in the middle and I was on the nearest side where the telephone table was, to take my on-call emergency calls.

We fell asleep quite comfortably without further ado. About 45 minutes later the inevitable bleep went off and I picked up the telephone to answer it. There was a patient down in casualty with severe abdominal pain and light vaginal bleeding, with the possibility of an ectopic pregnancy. I told the sister I'd be on my way. I got out of bed and started getting dressed, at which point I heard a squeak from Debbie. "What's the matter?" I said. She squeaked again and then rapidly got out of bed. "For goodness sake, Debbie, don't wake up Paul. What's the matter?" I reiterated. "I thought that was your hand massaging my bottom for the last 45 minutes", she gasped.

On my way down to casualty I was distracted from Paul's ungracious behaviour when I bumped into the obstetric SHO. She told me about a pregnant patient, who had brought herself up to labour ward because her husband had got her all worried.

She was still sniggering to the midwife when I asked, "Please let me share your amusement?" The SHO looked at me, trying franticly to keep a straight face and said, "This lady was at home lying on her tummy and was about 22 weeks pregnant. Her husband came in and said, "For god's sake Marilyn, stop lying on your tummy, you'll suffocate the poor little sod. Go on, open your legs and let him breathe!"

Once again the unmistakable truth about blokes and their complete ignorance of even basic female anatomy came to mind. As I pondered this thought, the timeless joke about this very subject flashed through my brain . . . .

What is the difference between a pub and a clitoris? The answer is . . . most blokes know their way to the Pub!

Chapter 17
How Not To Take A Professional Medical Exam

Since I can remember, my only ambition following graduation from medical school was to be become a general practitioner. I had no aims or aspirations as grand as my colleagues, who sat around me on those dissecting tables during those first two grim preclinical years. I remember Steve Jettison wanted to become anaesthetist and Glyn Keloid wanted to become a cardio-thoracic surgeon. I was certain that Nazi-Steve wanted to be a surgeon and Paul Sydney was definitely lined up for general surgery.

Ivan Baltimore wanted to become an orthopaedic surgeon, Steve Chimebells, I think, like me wanted to be a general practitioner and other notable recollections were Henrietta, who I think wanted to become an anaesthetist and gorgeous Kathy probably wanted to do paediatrics. At the hostel I remember my dear friend Andy ("I'm new") had his heart set on cardiology or something similarly exotic.

Those dreadful years in the anatomy dissecting room left me feeling completely numb when it came to any aspirations regarding activity in the operating theatre. After all, how could I possibly be of any use as a surgeon, if I was struggling so hard with the trials and tribulations of learning literally thousands of names, pathways and roadmaps all over the human body! As I have mentioned previously, I was so bad at anatomy that I acquired the new nickname of 'Gamma James'. With these credentials how could I possibly hope to embark upon a career more adventurous than general practice!

Anyway, to cut a long story short, I muddled my way through medical school and qualification. I then went through my house jobs and had the amazing good fortune of being able to do not only my house jobs in professorial departments, but also my senior house officer posts. This brings me to the part of my story, where I thought that I would see the light at the end of the tunnel pointing towards my career in general practice. In those days, one had to do a certain number of jobs that were in keeping with a career in general practice and the ideal ones included obstetrics and gynaecology and paediatrics.

I had reached the obstetric phase in my training and had enjoyed a six-month attachment at the West London Hospital working for marvellous bosses like Michael Portion and Galion Sym who were such charming gentleman from the 'old school'. The professor of the department was also known to my dad, when he was a lecturer at the same hospital in the old building some 15 years before. He was a very kind and affable man and he alone, was responsible for my demise, making me end up in the specialty I find myself in today!

The West London was a delightful 'touchy-feely' sort of place, making itself very prominent in the new climate and culture of 'hands on' obstetrics, where everybody had to be involved. The fathers were actively encouraged to take part in the labour process, rubbing their wife's backs and massaging them throughout the difficult moments of labour. Some were even encouraged to cut the umbilical cord as a means of helping to bond with the baby. Other fathers took things a little bit too far and slept with their wives in the same bed after the delivery. Some even took home the afterbirth, so that they could pan fry it for supper! Charles Leboyer, from a famous French institute was a regular visitor and lecturer to our department. We all knew what the meaning of natural childbirth was.

We were all sucked into this new culture of obstetrics, where the midwife was destined to take over and leave us poor obstetricians very much out of the limelight, waiting in the wings for our turn to do something useful.

In this cosy climate, where the poor patients had no personal secrets from the staff, we would revel in the departmental psychosexual meetings. Here we would discuss, in great detail, the psychosexual social history of our patients in relation to anticipating how well they would deal with their new offspring. I gleefully remember interrogating one of these poor mothers on the antenatal ward because there was a suspicion that she might be depressed. I relished the moment when I was able to tell the gathering of senior consultants, registrars, SHOs, midwives and psychologists (not to mention any members of any other medical establishment within the hospital) about my findings concerning this poor woman.

I was able to reveal that the reason she was depressed and withdrawn was because she hadn't been able to tell her husband that their previous baby was not indeed by him, but by another man with whom she had a casual fling on a business trip. Moreover she had divulged to me the history of being sexually abused as a child. I knew this would lead to a feeding frenzy of debate amongst all the healthcare professionals involved in this rather bizarre gathering.

I remember having just described this poor woman's history, there followed the most enormous discussion which went on for nearly 45 minutes. At the end of it, we as a group, became very confident about how we were going to go about making her feel so much better about this pregnancy and the eventual outcome! Despite our efforts, I believe this particular lady had postnatal depression, which was so severe that she had to be admitted to a local psychiatric institute. She also got divorced after her husband left her and lost custody of the children! What a result!

Anyway, it appeared to my professor's mind, that I was actively participating in his firm and obviously enjoying the job, so it wasn't too surprising that one day I was summoned to his office. At first I thought I was in trouble, but after I had walked into his office, which was in the annexe of an old converted West London house just outside the ancient building of the hospital itself, I thought that there wasn't going to be any problem. "Sit down", he said, "I've got something to show you."

There was a heap of letters in front of him and my first emotion was that of a feeling of dread that these were all letters of complaint, from patients who had taking exception to my rather frivolous, overconfident and perhaps even cocky approach to my work! After all, I was very confident, thinking that I was marvellous because of all the prestigious jobs that I had bagged at the hospital. To my mind there appeared to be very little difficulty in obtaining them! After all, even my dad said he didn't know anybody who had done two professorial house jobs at their own teaching hospital, let alone two professorial SHO jobs!

The professor pointed out to me that these letters were all complimentary about me and came from a variety of grateful patients, including those from the lower social economic classes. Not the usual toffs who frequented the West London, following recommendations made in Vogue magazine and the Good Birthing Guide. "James", he said, "These patients have gone to a lot of trouble to write to me about you and I think it is my duty to let you know that you would be very welcome in this specialty and I would like to encourage you to join us, in the form of an 'embryo obstetrician'.

I had difficulty in keeping a straight face when this excellent play on words popped out of the mouth of the professor of obstetrics. Nevertheless, I was still quite streetwise in those days and appreciated the fact that every six months a junior doctor was looking for another job. I felt it was quite likely that I was on the brink of being offered another six months contract. The professor went on; "If you would like to consider my proposal seriously I'm prepared to offer you another six months working as an SHO in gynaecology." I thought about this proposition for the whole of at least one nano-second and said, "Thank you professor, I'd be delighted."

Shortly afterwards I finished my day's work and went out to the pub to celebrate with my friends Nazi-Steve and Steven Chimebells. That night when I returned to my room in Cliff House on the 13th floor, overlooking the Thames estuary, I found a little envelope that had been slipped under my door. I opened it and found the inevitable green stationery of the Royal College of Obstetricians and Gynaecologists, laying out the guidance and regulations on how to take the first part of the Membership examination of the Royal College. My heart sank. It was quite obvious, the professor was being serious, and now I had plugged myself into my first post-graduate professional examination.

I decided to take this effort seriously, thinking that I had nothing to lose and if I changed my mind later it wouldn't matter too much anyway. How wrong I was. Had I any idea of the grief and anguish that this 'Part 1' examination was going to cause me over the next 18 months, I would have run a mile like a scalded cat straight out of the front door of the hospital and safely back to my world of cosy (no further examinations) general practice.

In all fairness, I think I took my first go at the MRCOG Part 1 quite seriously. As far as studying was concerned I started early enough, read the correct text books, consulted with other students who had done the examination, and pushed myself to do at least two hours of reading every evening in the three months leading up to the exam. I even took formal study leave for the two weeks before the examination and went to Leicester to my parent's, home where I had a period of potentially undisturbed studying time. This would also include losing the distraction of my girlfriend Debbie who remained in London.

I vividly remember riding up to Leicester on my Honda CBX, with quite a heavy rucksack full of textbooks, in the early part of September 1984. There are things about this fortnight that clearly stick in my mind. First of all, I wasn't alone in the house as both of my brothers were there. Looking back I'm not really sure why they were there in the first place. Hugh had already qualified as a doctor and I remember he was doing postgraduate examinations but I cannot recall him swotting with me at the time. PJ, who was still at polytechnic in Kingston, was also swotting. But I do remember the fact that my parents were away on a cruise.

We, therefore, had the perfect opportunity to use the house as a bachelor pad and envisaged having the time of our lives should we have felt the need. I cannot recall this happening however. I was studying quite seriously on a day-to-day basis and there wasn't much in the way of partying going on. Having said that, things got off to a good start (as far as the revision process was concerned) and one day I thought that I might just go for a short break after a particularly tedious morning trying to understand (as well as memorise) the intricate anatomy of the female pelvis. To this day I'm still not sure where all the branches of the internal iliac artery are!

I took my beautiful six cylinder Honda out of the garage for a quiet spin across the countryside and down towards one of the local villages. It was a Wednesday afternoon and my treat was to pick up the weekly copy of Motorcycle News. My plan was to bring it back, have a cup of tea, enjoy reading the articles for a while and then resume my swotting. I remember going to the news-agents and looking at the front page of this newspaper and seeing the most glorious picture of the latest generation of four cylinder Kawasaki Super Bikes. For me, it all started in the mid seventies with the Kawasaki 900 four pipe, simply called the Z900. This was every schoolboy's dream bike and it had dwarfed the Honda CB750 Four, which we had all lusted after the year previously.

The new generation Z bike was just the 'dog's bollocks' as far as everybody was concerned. It was now 1984 and Kawasaki had released the next monster in the form of the GPZ 1100. I looked at the photograph and read the headline underneath. It simply specified, "The new GPZ1100: 150 miles an hour at your fingertips." I just had to have one! I took the newspaper home and read the article on the GPZ at least a dozen times, showing my brother Hugh who also enthused about how marvellous it was. The next thing I discovered was that a whole afternoon of swotting was being completely wasted, as I rode my Honda into Leicester to the newly opened Kawasaki dealership just outside the town centre.

Needless to say, the showroom had the latest GPZ 1100 lined up with its other new Super Bike sister called the GPZ 900 water-cooled. I took both brochures home with me and after drooling over these motorcycles for at least one and a half hours, I reflected on the fact that I had also grilled the poor shop assistant into the ground about the merits of both these fabulous machines!

Caught in a Flap!

Instead of swotting that evening, I pored over the brochures, comparing and contrasting these two machines. Should I have the traditional air-cooled 1100 with brute horsepower or the more streamlined water-cooled more nimble and modern 900 with the major disadvantage of having a smaller engine? To resolve this agony, I discussed it with my brother Hugh in enormous detail, using the facilities of our local pub and its reputation for real ale to make the decision-making process even more enjoyable.

By the next morning I had my heart set on a GPZ 1100 and I could think of nothing else. My swotting had been blown out of the water and the only way this situation could be resolved was by having one! The next day, I wasted another completely useful session of swotting by doing frantic negotiations with my bank manager and various other loan companies, with a view to trying to procure the funds to get this machine.

I remember getting a pitiful part exchange on my splendid six cylinder Honda not to mention a ridiculously high interest rate for the loan to buy the Kawasaki. Eventually, the machine was delivered to me just shortly before the end of my first week's swotting. Looking back, this was the most ridiculous thing I have ever done whilst preparing for an exam. How can anybody swot sensibly, knowing that there is the brand new machine of one's dreams sitting in the garage directly underneath where you are swotting?

At every opportunity I was out for a ride on this lovely bike. The enjoyment of all these rides was always tainted by a feeling of guilt about buying the bike too early and not waiting until after I had done the exam. If this distraction wasn't bad enough there was worse yet to come. Just when I thought that I was getting over the excitement of my new machine and some semblance of normal revision activity was once again taking place, I got some correspondence from my best friend Phil in Zimbabwe.

He was doing a 'lightning trip' over to England, following a sabbatical from Harare to Sweden. He wanted to see me for a few days before he returned to Africa. I knew that the sensible thing to say was "no" because I was in the middle of some serious revision, but on the other hand, Phil was my best friend and it would be thrilling to see him for the weekend. I arranged with Debbie for Phil to stay with us in

Debbie's tiny bed-sit in Chiswick and I also arranged to pick up Phil from the airport. I remember leaving Leicester at about 4 o'clock in the morning, having had absolutely no sleep the night before, because I was so excited. I drove down to meet him in the early hours of Saturday morning at Heathrow and took him straight over to Debbie's flat.

We had a marvellous reunion night out, including the usual festivities at our local ESB pub on the Chiswick High Road, followed by the inevitable hot curry. I spent the whole of Sunday with him and we had a marvellous day out visiting all the local sites. It was great to see Debbie again even though it was a week earlier than I had planned. I can remember using our favourite expression of "We really tore the arse out of that weekend" when I said goodbye to Phil at the airport on Sunday night. It had been a truly exhausting session throughout and I remember nearly falling asleep at the wheel on my drive back to Leicester in my lovely lilac blue Daimler.

On returning to Leicester, I only had a few days left to prepare for this examination and I recall thinking how many hours I had wasted on motorcycle purchases and frivolous nights out, when really, I should have been studying for the exam. Another week of half-hearted swotting followed usually interrupted by the irresistible rides on my demonic red motorcycle. The week gradually came to a close and I made my next fatal pre-examination mistake.

I went back to Debbie's bed-sit on Sunday evening, the night before the examination but really, had I been sensible, should have gone back to my digs at the hospital. When I drove down, I was still not convinced that I had done enough work and felt that I wasn't at all prepared to take this examination. Those misgivings soon evaporated when I saw Debbie's pretty face and found myself back in the cosy smoky atmosphere of the Pack Horse & Talbot Fuller's ESB pub.

I promised myself that I would have only a moderate amount of alcohol and retire early. Some hope! After four pints of ESB, I found myself in the local tandoori restaurant ordering my usual favourite meat vindaloo, plain rice, papadoms, sag aloo and hot lime pickle sauce. This was more like a Saturday night binge rather than the serious evening before one's first truly professional post-graduate examination!

Caught in a Flap!

I can clearly recall falling into Debbie's bed-sit very close to midnight, feeling the inevitable consequences of our drunken evening. It was great lying in that tiny room listening to our favourite Fleetwood Mac music while the Scottish guy in the room above did his very best to keep in time by playing 'The Cry of the Valcaries' at full volume, whilst using his pelvis thrusts as a source of extra rhythm! We giggled relentlessly about his performance and when his girlfriend let fly with a truly appreciative orgasm, we offered a very loud applause from down below. After a brief pause he shouted through the floorboards, in a broad Glaswegian accent, "Hey Jimmie you's should try this sometime!"

Eventually I fell into a fitful flatulent sleep, only to wake up at half-past one in the morning, belching and feeling totally dehydrated with a splitting headache! I can remember that night vividly, because I didn't go back to sleep. God, there was a terrible smell of vindaloo flavoured curry farts and stale cigarette smoke, not to mention beery breath! At a rough guess I think I tossed and turned, farting and belching like blokes do, at least a thousand times. I got up for at least three trips to the lavatory to relieve myself and remembered what a 'Flaming A' felt like.

The thing that I can recall most vividly is Debbie's radio alarm clock's fluorescent dial burning deeply into my retina showing me the numbers 3 am, 3.15 am, 3.25 am, 4 am, and so on, all through the night. I was literally opening my eyes every ten to fifteen minutes to have a look to see what the time was! That was the most fitful night I can ever remember and to cut a long story short, when the alarm did go off at seven fifteen, I had only just dropped off to sleep before that agonising moment!

I dragged myself into the shower feeling absolutely ragged. I was hung over, exhausted and reeking of curry and Fuller's ESB. I was in a dreadful mood and felt absolutely awful about myself and realising again, how completely unprepared for this examination I was. Debbie kindly drove me in her massive Citroen CX 2.4 litre, long-wheel base French saloon and I remember thinking how completely over the top this car was for such a diminutive driver like herself.

She drove me all the way to the Royal College in Regents Park and dropped me off with a good luck kiss. I staggered into the exam hall some moments later feeling quite nauseous and very unsure of myself!

Caught in a Flap!

I listened to the usual dreary repertoire from the invigilators, telling us what pencils to use and how to mark our answer sheets correctly. There was the prospect of a forthcoming barrage of MCQ questions set over two long papers; one in the morning and one in the afternoon.

I hated MCQ examinations at the best of times and here I found myself really vulnerable given the previous night's events. Eventually the inevitable words, "You may begin", came over the public address system of the examination hall and I opened my paper to look at question one. I can remember the contents of this question as if it was yesterday. I can also remember what came afterwards.

The question said; "During the female orgasm the vagina contracts a) every one second b) every third of a second c) every two seconds d) every point seven of a second e) every five seconds." I looked through my bloodshot eyes at the examination question over and over again. I contemplated my terrible headache, my smelly breath, my perspiration and my overall feeling of making a complete 'balls' of the whole of the swotting process during the previous two weeks.

There and then, I decided to make some kind of stand. I lifted up my HB pencil and instead of filling in one of the lozenges to mark my answer, I wrote on the examination sheet next to the question. "I do not know the answer to this question, because I do not have an eye on the end of my knob!"

I left the examination hall at about 6 pm and as I staggered down the stairs of the entrance of the Royal College of Obstetricians and Gynaecologists, I reflected on the fact that there weren't many things that were absolutely dead certain in my life, but one thing was for sure. I would be back to take this examination again! And again! I was right. I required another two appearances before I was able to get over that particular hurdle in my career.

And guess what! The answer is; "Every point seven of a second"!

Chapter 18
Come Again!

Goodness how times have changed. I've just finished the consultant ward round on delivery suite and have seen the registrar, who was on call last night, going home to have a really long sleep, before coming back tonight at 9 pm and taking over to do another shift. When I was a registrar a day at work started at 8:30 am. It was usually an ordinary day at work, perhaps with an operating theatre list in the morning and an antenatal clinic in the afternoon.

Then when it got to 5 pm you would present yourself to the delivery suite and look after the labour ward, with hardly any sleep, all night until 9 am the next morning. Then the whole cycle would start again, with perhaps another clinic or an operating list that morning. When it got to 5 pm you'd start thinking about getting ready to go home and if you were lucky, at around about 6 to 6:30 pm you would have finished all your ward work, got on your motorcycle and headed off home.

More often than not, you would decide when you got home, that you were so incredibly knackered after the previous night's stint on the delivery, suite that you might just have a little hour's snooze before you went out to see your friends. A little nap on the settee before having a 'shit, shower and a shave' would be a very reasonable option.

However there was one major disadvantage. Sadly that little hour's snooze would frequently turn into a full night's sleep and you'd wake up the next morning, not only with the misery of realising you missed your night out, but also the horrible inevitability of being on call again that very same day! There is nothing more depressing than arriving on the delivery suite knowing that you missed your night out and you're going to be stuck in the hospital again for another 32 hours!

During my training as a middle-grade doctor, there was however some respite in the form of quite a civilised rota. This meant that when we were working on the delivery suite in a North London hospital, we only had to do half weekend shifts. In other words instead of being there from 9 am Friday till 5 pm Monday, we only had to do a Saturday or a Sunday and not both. This obviously made life far more bearable, but nevertheless there was always something there to spoil it. On this occasion it was a diabetic patient whose labour was being induced.

She also happened to be a pet patient of my consultant and rumour had it that this was something to do with referring private patients! One Friday, early in the evening after a full day at work, I took over the delivery suite from the other registrar and got a handover about this patient, who was being personally looked after by our consultant Miss Thomas.

Miss Thomas had a special interest in this patient who happened to be a doctor. Dr Purcell had a difficult obstetric history and more importantly, her diabetic condition had needed very careful management during her previous labours. Miss Thomas had already approached me on previous occasions saying that she was planning an induction of labour for Dr Purcell and that should I be on duty and Dr Purcell was in, I had to be there to take blood and measure the blood sugars every hour on the hour during labour. I had to make sure the doctor had the best possible standard of care.

The thought of getting up every hour during the night to measure a blood sugar was absolutely abhorrent to me and made me feel really uncomfortable about doing the labour ward on call. It was difficult enough to snatch a few hours sleep anyway, without the realisation of knowing that you would be woken up every hour regardless. I took on this duty as I had no other choice. I remember my chirpy colleague, who gave me the handover, sniggering as he left the ward, knowing that I was going to have a lousy night.

Needless to say, despite our efforts to induce Dr Purcell and my getting up every hour to do her blood sugars, nothing happened and she still hadn't delivered the next morning. In fact, it is fair to say that her uterus was probably quiescent all night and all our efforts to induce her had been a total failure. Anyway it was 9 am Saturday morning and at least I could go home.

I handed over her care to the chirpy registrar, who was a bit disappointed that she hadn't delivered, but also quite cheerful in the knowledge that we would probably be giving her a day off from further intervention. This was so that she could rest before starting another trial of induction the next day.

Caught in a Flap!

The inevitable happened. On Sunday morning, when I arrived back at the hospital, I found that Dr Purcell had had her 24 hour break and was now going to be induced again. Predictably, it was once again my brief to do her hourly blood sugars throughout the night! "Oh bollocks," I thought. It was a very busy day on the delivery suite and lots of mothers were having their babies. In the background of all this activity I religiously was able to make sure that Dr Purcell's blood sugars were taken every hour for the optimal management of her diabetes.

The next morning I was delighted to report that Dr Purcell had delivered a little baby boy perfectly safely and there had been no mishaps and her blood sugar monitoring had been perfect throughout the night.

After breakfast I went to do my usual ward rounds. On arrival at the postnatal ward, I was greeted by a very distraught-looking sister and a student midwife who was crying. "What's the matter?" I said to the sister. "Dr James", she said, "something very grave has happened and I need to discuss this with you immediately". "Of course", I said, "What has been the problem?" "Well," the sister began, "do you know who

Dr Purcell is?" "Of course I know who Dr Purcell is", I said, "she's kept me up for two nights looking after her blood sugars, on the hour every hour, throughout the bleeding weekend", I exclaimed! "What on earth has happened? All I know is that she successfully delivered a baby boy and everybody was happy."

"Well, I'm not happy", grumbled the sister, "and neither is my student midwife." "What on earth is the problem?" I asked, quite intrigued by this whole situation. "Well," said the sister, "we went on the routine drug round and entered Dr Purcell's side room and to our complete shock found her performing fellatio on her husband who was standing at her bedside! This has upset my student midwife enormously and I feel that this is a disgraceful situation." I could hardly contain myself. The whole thing sounded incredibly bizarre. "Don't worry, sister", I said trying franticly to keep a straight face, "I will report this to Miss Thomas, in no uncertain terms, on our afternoon ward round." "OK", said the sister, "but I do expect to get some feedback about this behaviour."

Later on that day the consultant ward round took place. The usual entourage of medical students were there and Miss Thomas, a diminutive little Welsh woman with high stiletto heels and a very rich Welsh accent, greeted me in the usual way by saying, "Hello Cariad, can we go round?"

"Of course we can, Miss Thomas," I replied.

"I've prepared all the patients for you and I'm happy to report what's happening."

"Before we go", she said," I believe that Dr Purcell had a baby this morning."

"Yes" I said. She took a deep breath and looked at me intensively; "Didn't we do well with Dr Purcell?" she said gushingly. I said, "Yes, Miss Thomas, we did very well with Dr Purcell. In fact, to show her appreciation of all the care that she had, she performed fellatio on her husband in front of the student midwife and the sister during the drug round this morning."

Miss Thomas looked at me in total disbelief. She took the most enormous intake of breath with her chest and breasts heaving upwards as she did so. "Come again?"

She shrieked. I looked at her penetratively and said, "That's what Dr Purcell said, Miss Thomas."

The ward round ended early that day.

Chapter 19
Larger Than Life

One of my favourite characters, as I look back on all of those happy years as a junior doctor, has to be the delightful, eccentric and outrageous Roger Greenblaum. Roger was an extremely talented, artistic Cambridge graduate who had a fantastic ability to write and participate in medical school reviews. In all fairness, I think his vocation should have been on the big screen or at least in theatre. However he had found his way into medicine and enriched the lives of all the people working around him, from the point of view of his magnificent sense of humour and larger than life character. Most important of all, was his ability to show absolutely no insight whatsoever into how outrageous his behaviour was!

He cut a fine figure and some would argue he was quite a handsome chap looking very similar, to my mind, to the actor Richard Gere. He had a shock of black hair, finely chiselled features and a voice reminiscent of a squadron leader. To make the squadron leader image even more realistic he used to fling himself around London in a tiny frog-eyed Austin Healy Sprite. He drove it wearing the head gear from a Second World War fighter plane. The sight of Roger in his minute sports car wearing his aviation goggles was really something to behold. This was particularly if he was dashing to an emergency and leaping out of the car and into the delivery suite, without even taking his goggles and helmet off!

Apart from this colourful and outrageous behaviour, there are two things that I warmly remember the squadron leader for. First was his outrageous behaviour on the ward rounds and secondly his completely unscrupulous nature when it came to other people's girl friends! Starting with the outrageous behaviour, I found myself as his senior house officer and he my registrar sometime in the mid eighties. He arrived on his first day at work and introduced himself to his new pair of SHOs.

He was very keen to lay down the rules and explained how he wanted his ship run. In particular, he was quite strict about the concept of regular ward rounds and keeping him informed of events at all times. He believed that if he could impress the consultant with a good working knowledge of all the patients, then this would obviously offer him some success with his career.

At this time obstetrics and gynaecology was still quite a competitive specialty and you needed all the help you could get, particularly that from your boss. This is where Roger was in a slightly difficult situation. His first boss at registrar level was Miss Corrigan and she herself had just been appointed as a very young consultant. In fact, she'd only just left the post of senior registrar at one of the big teaching hospitals. Even for a senior registrar, we thought she was very young and had done incredibly well up the career ladder.

There was obviously bound to be some kind of conflict with Roger's gregarious personality and Miss Corrigan's quite religious and strict upbringing as a single child in the Lake District. My opposite number on this firm was a chap called Robert Bog, who was about my age and had quite clear career intentions of becoming a successful obstetrician. Bob Bog was also quite a serious sort of chap and he used to smoke a pipe in the doctor's mess, even though he was only in his mid twenties. Having said that he was already married and I believe had a little girl at the time, so he was quite a few light years ahead of us in the maturity stakes anyway.

Squadron leader Greenblaum gradually settled in and within days it was time to do the first consultant ward round. Needless to say, Bob and I kept Roger filled in completely with what was going on with the patients and we had quite a rather busy post-take ward round to get through. Miss Corrigan came along, bright and breezy and cheerful as usual. We started the gynaecology ward round where had there been quite a few admissions from the night before. In the corner of the ward there was a quiet, sad looking young woman who was probably in her early twenties and had a very strong cockney accent.

She probably had quite a deprived upbringing. She had been admitted with a history of quite severe pelvic pain and obviously we were thinking along the lines of some kind of infection. Our consultant glanced over towards the patient way before we had actually started our ward round formally. "Roger", she said in a slightly subdued voice, "why does that young lady over in the corner look so sad?" Roger glanced over and acknowledged who the patient was. He then took in a deep breath and in a foghorn voice said, "Well boss, how would you feel if your 'Spade' boyfriend kicked the shit out of you every day?" Bob Bog and I nearly died with embarrassment!

We could not believe our ears. Our boss looked appropriately taken back but didn't comment too much. I think she was in too much of a state of shock to realise what had really happened! Nevertheless the ward round continued and eventually we reached the obstetric ward where there were quite a few patients waiting for decisions to be made about the delivery of their babies.

Roger's relentless form continued. We arrived at the bedside of a woman who obviously had an enormous baby. She herself was quite minute. Miss Corrigan, on consulting with Roger and taking some more history from the patient, decided that it would probably be in the best interest for this woman to have an elective caesarean section without the opportunity of going into labour. On announcing this management decision to the patient, Roger yelled with excitement and went,

"Chop, chop! I will sharpen the knives!" At this point Bob Bog and I glanced at the patient who looked physically sick, whilst an exasperated Miss Corrigan gazed up to the ceiling in a state of total disbelief.

Later on that afternoon, I found myself covering labour ward and we had a slight problem with a patient whose infant was very premature. A decision had been made at consultant level that we should really transfer this mother and her baby out to one of the big teaching hospitals. I had arranged for the senior registrar in paediatrics to come over from St Mary's with an ambulance and a support crew. The idea was that if the mother delivered in the ambulance, a senior doctor would be available to resuscitate the infant. I thought that it would be polite to tell Roger, who was the duty registrar, what the plan was. He said he'd come to the delivery suite immediately he had finished his clinic over at the other hospital down the road.

A little later on the senior registrar from St Mary's had arrived and I took it upon myself to introduce him to the patient and explain to her what was going to happen. We arrived in the delivery room in front of this rather apprehensive mother. Just as I was about to start introducing the senior registrar and explaining the situation, there was a squeal of tyres as a little frog-eyed Sprite came to a dramatic halt outside the delivery suite front door. Roger leapt out of the car, without opening the door and rushed into the front foyer straight towards the nursing station main desk. He leapt over the desk, rather than running around the edge of it and then burst through the swinging doors of the room that we were all assembled in. Then, complete with goggles and crash helmet, he clicked his fingers hard and shouted, "Story!"

The senior registrar looked at this spectacle in total disbelief. "Hello Roger", I said, "I'd like you to meet the senior registrar from St Mary's who has come to pick up this mother as an in-utero transfer." The two men looked at each other and the senior registrar said, "Interesting entrance." Roger replied dryly, "All part of the service my dear chap."

I really did enjoy working with Roger. Everyday there was always a really good laugh when he was about and sometimes he would do things that were unrelated to work that were equally outrageous.

On one occasion my girlfriend Debbie and I had returned from a trip to Africa. It was Debbie's first trip to Zimbabwe and being of a delicate constitution, I was not at all surprised that some vile African lergy would get the better of her. Needless to say, I was right and on the return flight I noticed that she was a little feverish and unwell. Two days back into England she was complaining of respiratory difficulty. Because of my on-call commitments in the hospital, I was forced to bring her with me to work one evening to see the casualty department doctors.

Debbie was admitted and put on the respiratory unit, while I continued with my night on call. However, in the morning they felt that she was well enough to be discharged, but of course there was nobody to take her home. I did the honourable thing and put her in my on-call room which I shared with Roger and the other lads. It was Roger's turn to be on call that night with a different SHO. As usual, he arrived in the on-call room to get changed ready for work. At that point, I had already vacated the room, leaving Debbie comfortably tucked up with a slice of toast and a cup of tea. I told her I'd be along to see her later on that morning.

Roger had arrived some five minutes after I'd left. He picked up the keys and went straight into the on-call room without knocking. He then saw this beautiful young thing sitting in the bed innocently munching her toast. The extraordinary part about this story is that he really failed to introduce himself properly. He simply burst into the room with his fresh theatre gear under his arm and then casually glanced at Debbie with a cursory, "Good Morning" and then started to take his clothes off to get changed.

At the point where he was standing in his underpants he glanced over to Debbie and said, "Who are you?" She said, "My name is Debbie." He said, "What are you doing in the on-call room?" She said, "I was admitted to the hospital last night and Mickey says I'm not well enough to go home on my own today, so he's going to leave me here and take me home this evening, when he has finished work."

Roger then says, "Are you feeling any better now?" She says, "Yes, a little bit." Then he started to put his top on and still standing in his underpants looked over again and then looked at his watch. Realising that it was only a quarter to nine, he turned around to her and said,

"Fancy a shag?" Debbie was absolutely exasperated. "Don't you know who I am?" she said. "Yes, you are Mike's girlfriend but I'm his registrar and all is fair in love and war you know", he said enthusiastically.

I like to think that Debbie declined Roger's kind offer and more interesting is the fact that he never ever mentioned this episode to me . . . . But thankfully, Debbie did.

Chapter 20
The Story Of The Green Ring Piece

My research years were lean ones. I had very little money, nowhere decent to live and my girlfriend had left me. Overall, I wasn't a very happy person. Being in my early thirties and living in the Irish nursing home in dreary North London was quite a pitiful and wretched existence. I could never really get used to sharing a bath with 24 other girls (not at once that is). There was always the trouble of cleaning out the previous person's mess and I got sick of the sight of pubic hairs blocking up the plughole. My room was the size of a shoe box, situated in a very gloomy end of the residence building at the hospital. It was safe to say that I was truly miserable.

If that wasn't bad enough, I had left all my research cameras and photographic equipment in the front of my car one night, which got broken into and all my belongings were stolen. So, on this particular day that I can remember, I was feeling pretty low as I walked down the hill to the hospital, which was about

20 minutes from the nursing home. During that time I pondered on my future and wondered what was in store for me during the day ahead.

I wasn't going to do a research clinic that morning as I was down for a simple NHS colposcopy clinic. The first patient came in looking pretty angry indeed. She was about 35 years old, and was wearing very plain clothes and had a very short haircut. I remember her having a ring through one of her nostrils. This was the time when body jewellery was just coming into vogue and my boss, the Prof always said that body jewellery was a particularly good marker for high risk of infection with the human papillomavirus, thought to cause cancer of the cervix.

My consultation with this woman was difficult. She was very brusque and abrasive, kept glaring at me and more importantly, seemed to resent my presence altogether. I tried to be as polite as possible, but she was nevertheless still difficult and contrary. Eventually, at one point during the consultation, I decided that the best thing to do was to get on and examine her, rather than continue a rather complicated and tedious history. I persuaded her, in the nicest possible way, to get onto the examination couch, so that I could look at her cervix with my microscope. She very reluctantly agreed and with the help of the sister, positioned herself accordingly. I started my examination and focused the microscope on her cervix. As I was doing this, she started a monologue of, "How, if it wasn't for men, she would never have found herself in this awful position in the first place."

She then went on to say that men were the route of all evil and as far as she was concerned, there wouldn't be any sexually-transmitted diseases if there weren't any men. I must admit, I thought she did have a point there! She continued to be rude about men in general and then started to say that if she had been able to avoid contact with men, she would never have got this awful disease. In fact, she said that everything horrible that had ever happened to her was all the fault of a man! What I did not know, however, was the history behind all this ill feeling.

It transpired later, whilst I was having a conversation with the colposcopy nurse, that this patient had every reason to be irritated. Apparently, she and her lesbian partner had decided to have a baby and the only way this could happen was for one of them to go to a party and find a man. Unfortunately the gentleman in question had given the prospective mother rather a bad cluster of genital warts, not to mention an abnormal smear! But I did not know this vital piece of information at the time of my examination, so I carried on as best I could!

I was beginning to feel a little bit lonely at the bottom end of the couch trying to find her cervix. Nevertheless, the tirade against the male species continued. Eventually, I had to think of a ploy to stop it. I moved my colposcope very delicately downwards towards her anal margin and put on the green filter and magnification up to about 100. What we saw on the television screen was an enormously enlarged anus, twitching as the woman was speaking. She glanced up at the TV screen in the middle of one of her tirades to be presented with this enormous green anus twitching in time with her own dialogue. "What's that?" she shrieked. "That's your anus", I said. "Why is it green?" she asked. "Because I put a green filter on so I can see the anatomy and architecture of your tissues in better detail", I answered. "Why is it twitching?" she asked.

"Because you're talking", I said. All of a sudden she went very quiet.

I felt that I was suddenly developing some kind of rapport with this woman, as she softened and had a much more friendly conversation. I refocused my camera on her cervix, put the standard filter on and started to examine. She happened to become intrigued with the quality of the picture and the resolution of detail that I was showing her. "That's rather a jolly good picture" she said. "What's that pattern I can see on my cervix?" I explained to her what I was looking at and its implications in terms of disease.

She then went on to say that such a good quality picture really enabled her to understand what was happening. I couldn't resist the temptation and took a deep breath and said, "It's got to be a good quality picture because there are 200 medical students watching this in the lecture theatre!" I looked at her horrified expression for two nanoseconds and then said, just like the famous comedian Harry Enfield, "Only joking!"

Chapter 21
All Mouth And No Trousers

As a junior registrar I had several hysterical experiences, which usually involved being on call at the hospital, but sometimes very funny things happened outside the usual working hours. As was so typical of the time, one of my hospitals was very keen on enjoying the festive season. This applied across all of the departments and Christmas time was literally associated with trying a different departmental party every night for the 10 days or so building up to Christmas itself.

The midwives party was pretty spectacular. As we had a high contingent of West Indian midwives, a lot of delicious catering effort went into making the feast for the party. As a result there was a wide variety of exotic Indian and Caribbean dishes, including jerk chicken and lovely curries. Everybody joined in. The midwives brought food and doctors brought drinks. Everyone was invited and it was one of those really lovely evenings that left most people with quite serious hangovers. Thankfully, the party was usually on a Friday night, so at least most of us had a chance to recover without facing another working day.

There was one party in particular I remember. It was during a time where I developed the deepest infatuation with what I can only describe as a beautiful young midwife, who was completely unobtainable as she was married to a police officer. The attraction of this fair-skinned, dark-haired beauty was the fact that she used to model underwear in the catalogues for some of the big chain stores. This immediately made her deliciously attractive as far as I and all my other randy young registrar friends were concerned.

Not only did she have a beautiful face, but also a fantastic figure in keeping with her other occupation. She regularly used to accompany me on ward-rounds and particularly on weekends, when it was just she and I together I would often fantasise about her accompanying me down to medical records to look for an elusive set of patient notes.

I would imagine her lying on top of the notes trolley wearing this spectacular underwear, being pushed backwards and forwards against me between rows of filing cabinets. Anyway, enough of that, let's move on to the party.

It was the Christmas of 1985 I believe and all the midwives had made the usual preparations in the main lounge of the Irish nursing home. The bar was open, the drinks were flowing and there was a huge turnout of hospital staff. I remember that even most of the consultants had attended, which was something quite unusual for a hospital party. I still have all the photographs of me dancing with all the midwives en masse. This was obviously a very safe thing for a young man to do when one's girlfriend was working in another hospital!

My brother Paul had been invited with the prospect of meeting lots of young midwives. I was standing at the bar with him, drinking a pint of Stella Artois and enjoying a cigarette. By this time it was quite late into the evening and I was feeling a little the worse for wear but nevertheless still enjoying the atmosphere. I was without my girlfriend that night because Debbie was working on a nightshift at another hospital.

As I discussed the evening's activities with my brother there was a slight tap on my left shoulder. I turned round and there she was; the beautiful midwife with the fantastic undies. "Hello", I said, all enthusiastic to see her. She was a little bit sloshed, but nevertheless pretty composed. "Hello, Mike", she said. "Are you enjoying yourself?"

Before I could answer she went on in a more serious voice. "Michael", she said, "Have you got the key to your on-call room?" "Yes", I said rather nervously. She took a deep breath and her gaze penetrated deep into my eyeballs. "I'd like you to take me to the on-call room . . . and make passionate love to me . . . , now."

She said it so slowly and clearly that there was absolutely no mistaking what she meant! A wave of overwhelming panic struck me and the concept of 'all talk and no trousers' hit me like a ton of bricks. In a fit of peak I replied in an almost a castrato style voice, "I can't!"

"Why not?" she said looking quietly disturbed. "Well I can't . . . because . . . because I've got eczema on my willy." My brother nearly suffocated in his pint, choking uncontrollably and splattering Stella Artois all over the bar. I looked back at her. She had gone.

Chapter 22
The Incredible 'Mr Smooth'

One of my fondest memories as a junior doctor was having the pleasure to work for Mr Trebor Studd. The reason I enjoyed working with him so much was because he was so smooth. He had a marvellous silky voice and used to smoke Rothman's King Size cigarettes, as well as sail a substantial yacht. He was a member of the Royal Navy Reserve I believe. His Jag had an outrageous bright turquoise paint job!

Mr Studd believed everything should be done in ship-shape fashion. He also had the most marvellous laid back attitude about life in general. It was not uncommon for him to arrive for the operating list round about 11.30 in the morning, having let the juniors get on with the work themselves. This was obviously thrilling for us, being allowed to operate in a relatively unsupervised environment and gave us great confidence for minor procedures.

Caught in a Flap!

He was also brilliant to the patients, but the thing I remember most was his ability to go completely against the grain. If a patient was irritating him he would certainly let her know in no uncertain terms! This we found refreshing. As I reflect on today's climate where we find ourselves literally grovelling to patients and their families, I have a very fond memory of those times when you could speak your mind and get away with it!

His ward rounds were always a pleasure, as there was often an interesting discussion or debate at the bedside of each and every patient. If he thought your management of a patient was below par, he would certainly let you know and as a result of this you always knew where you stood. It was the sense of knowing exactly where you stood, which probably saved me from the serious repercussions of one of the most memorable pranks I have ever had the privilege of undertaking!

I recall this episode as vividly as if it happened yesterday. I and the registrar 'Frog Eye-Sprite' were in theatre starting Mr Studd's list. It was the usual selection of diagnostic laparoscopies and dilatation with curettage. Mr Studd wouldn't let us do anything particularly difficult until he arrived. In fact, on reflection I don't think he let us do anything difficult at all as he seemed to enjoy operating himself so much! Around about midday, Mr Studd was well into the first major operation on his list and was finding it quite taxing, doing a hysterectomy on a patient with enormous fibroids on her uterus. Access was difficult in this large woman and clearly this case was going to take a little bit longer than planned.

Roger was assisting him as I'd been told to take a little break. At that point the sister in theatre walked in and announced that Mr Studd was needed on the telephone to speak to the sister from the gynaecology ward about one of his patients. I immediately offered to take the call as I was unscrubbed and obviously available. "That would be most kind", he said in his silky smooth voice.

I went immediately to the nursing station and picked up the telephone. I couldn't resist it. I just had to do my famous Trebor Studd voice impersonation, which I had been practising to perfection. "Hello sister", I said in a rather flirtatious drawl. The sister obviously thought this was Mr Studd and gushingly responded.

I could hear her almost sighing with anticipation on the other end of the telephone line. She gasped, "Oh Mr Studd, I'm so sorry to trouble you, but I felt it was very important to tell you that your patient has arrived on the ward. You know, the one that you especially wanted to see preoperatively."

I just couldn't resist it. I took a deep breath and said in a charming manner, "Thank you sister. Have I ever told you that I think you have magnificent breasts?" There was a stunned silence followed by an even louder gasp, "Oh Mr Studd", she responded with an attack of the vapours. I then continued, "Furthermore sister, I have to say, it would give me enormous pleasure to caress them." At this point the sister was too exasperated and hung up. I put the phone down and suddenly realised the true gravity of what I had done!

I rushed back into theatre and asked Mr Studd if it was alright if went upstairs to see if I could sort out the problem the sister had contacted him about. Obviously he agreed. I ran up the stairs to the ward and found sister in the coffee room looking a little bit apprehensive. She was an attractive woman in her early fifties. I believe she was from Ireland and it was quite likely, according to my other junior colleagues, that she'd had a crush on Mr Studd ever since he'd been a junior house officer working in the same hospital. "Cor, Sister Donning", I said, "didn't Mr Studd come on a bit strong?"

She gasped in absolute amazement. "Goodness", she said, "you didn't hear that conversation did you?" "Of course I did", I said, "We were all listening together in the coffee room." "Oh God", she uttered, "what am I going to do?" I then said, "You should really lay back and enjoy it!" Sister glared at me fiercely, so I decided to leave.

On returning to theatre, I had the sudden feeling of overwhelming panic. This sort of behaviour could easily be reported to higher authorities and I could easily be given a disciplinary warning or even be sacked. I decided to come clean and tell Mr Studd what had happened. "Mr Studd, I think you should know about the conversation I had with sister when I offered to take your call." "Go on", he said, in his typically smooth manner.

"Well, Mr Studd, I'm afraid I pretended I was you because I can do your voice rather well." "Go on", he said again. "Well, essentially, I said I thought that sister had great breasts and I would like to caress them." "Go on", he said showing an obvious flicker of interest. "Well, I thought I'd better tell you about her reaction." "Go on", he said. "Well, to tell you the truth she didn't seem to be too put out about it", I said lying through my teeth. Mr Studd looked at me quizzically and said, "Of course she didn't . . . . That's because I do it all the time."

"There IS a God," I thought when I left theatres and got on my motorcycle to make my way back to the obstetric hospital.

Chapter 23
The Case Of The Vanishing Finger

One of the thrills of being a junior obstetric registrar, in a prestigious teaching hospital setting, was that there was always an audience for you to try to impress. On this particular occasion, on a rather busy on-call weekend, it was my pleasure to demonstrate in front of medical students and several very attractive young student midwives, the art of repairing a perineal tear.

This very pleasant Irish woman had had a rather explosive delivery of her eighth child and the infant had given the mother a measurable degree of damage in the nether regions. In fact it would have been reasonable to describe the area as if a hand grenade had gone off in her vagina! Nevertheless, I was prepared to execute a masterful repair in front of the gathered audience.

The sister was very keen for her midwives to see repairs of this nature, as we were just entering the era where midwives were about to be trained to repair their own episiotomies. Similarly, the medical students were all eager to have first hand experience of the labour ward and were just about to embark upon their first deliveries.

There was a very quiet atmosphere in that gloomy labour ward room. It was approximately 11.30 at night and the lady's husband had been able to rush over to the local public house and squeeze in a few pints to celebrate the birth of Seamus.

Over the next 25 minutes, I took my audience through a detailed repertoire of surgical manoeuvres, illustrating the principles of correct skin apposition, haemostasis and avoidance of unnecessary tissue trauma. I also showed them the correct way to offer local anaesthesia and infiltrate the tissue in such a manner that the mother hardly noticed any surgery was going on.

As the tissue edges came together and normal anatomy was being restored, I could hear the gasps of admiration behind me. To finish my act, I had to perform a delicate examination to demonstrate to everybody that all the relevant anatomy was intact and back in one piece.

I paused momentarily and then said to the lady, "Excuse me Mrs Murphy, I need to insert my finger into your back passage." There was a subdued silence, followed by the emergence of a mysterious hand from underneath her right buttock. Her index finger gyrated like a worm trying to explore its bolt-hole. Eventually, the tip of her finger reached her anal margin and the entire finger vanished up into her bottom.

Taken aback I gasped, "What are you doing, Mrs Murphy?" There was a pause followed by, "Doctor, you told me to stick my finger up my ass." I slumped back in my operating chair in absolute amazement and I heard the husband say in a broad Belfast accent,

"Be-Jesus Mary, but you're tik."

Chapter 24
Crabs On Steroids

My little girls ask me to tell them some stories about what it was like living in Africa and I mainly concentrate on my childhood, but of course there was a whole other chunk of history associated with my frequent return trips to Rhodesia when it changed to Zimbabwe, following my graduation from medical school in the summer of 1980.

This story starts with a rather sad beginning, because it reminds me of the terrible disappointment I experienced one warm afternoon at the hospital in the autumn of 1980. Although I had qualified first time (which was quite a remarkable achievement for me) I did not apply for a house job straightaway like most of my contemporaries. The reason for this was that I wanted some time out after five years of hard graft at medical school.

My real ambition was to buy a huge motorcycle and go on a trip around Europe. I had recently split up with my girlfriend Debbie B, prior to qualifying. I was quite keen on finding a new girlfriend, as any hot-blooded young man would be. I could not stop thinking about the love of my life, Jennifer, the one that truly got away! For some strange reason I found her address buried under a pile of paperwork and swotting notes, in my bedroom at our small house in Liverpool. I took a wild chance and dropped her a line stating that I would love to see her again. I said that I had great plans about a marvellous motorcycle trip across Europe and how great it would be if she could come along too.

To my absolute amazement, Jenny wrote back almost immediately and said that, for some reason, she had also been thinking about me when my letter arrived. This was truly an astonishing coincidence, but more importantly, Jenny was very keen on the idea of coming over to England from Cape Town. She had never been to Europe and found the whole idea of a motorcycle adventure very exciting. I could hardly contain myself at this point. I was absolutely thrilled with the news and immediately went about preparing our trip.

I had the most amazing fantasies about Jennifer and me, romantically embracing each other on a topless beach somewhere in St Tropez and then going on to the casino that evening. This would be followed by a grand dinner in one of those seaside restaurants, where they sell tiger prawns the size of crabs and the aroma of garlic and white wine entrench the entire atmosphere.

I think it is fair to say that I was so excited about this trip; I could hardly sleep that night when the letter arrived. However there is a very sad ending to this story. About two weeks later, a letter arrived with a South African postmark on it. It was very brief and contained one photograph. The photograph, I am sad to say was a beautiful picture of Jennifer wearing a white wedding dress and cutting a cake. I was absolutely choked.

Apparently she had got back together with her old boyfriend and they had decided to get married rather quickly. Maybe he thought that if he hesitated again, she would be gone forever. I still have that photo of Jenny. Strangely and worryingly, it appears to be the only image that I have ever had of her. In particular I cannot remember us being photographed together.

I made numerous trips back to Zimbabwe after I qualified, the first one probably being the most memorable, as I had not seen the country for at least six years. I was a senior house officer and was able to get a really good flight out to Harare with a local airline. I clearly remember helping the African woman, sitting next to me, cut up her meat because she hadn't used a knife and fork before. I even had to help her open those peculiar containers that they serve on airlines and show her the difference between the butter and the milk. In those days, you could smoke on an aeroplane (which sounds absolutely outrageous now) and the back of the aircraft was thick with a smog of grey smoke, where all the loyal Rhodesians were still supporting their local thriving tobacco industry.

My first trip back to Harare was very exciting; as there were so many people I had not seen for so long, waiting to greet me at the airport. I prepared myself for a really boozy two-week holiday in the intensely entertaining environment of Phil Heath's mess. A mess was a place where young bachelors all lived together and Phil had four inmates in his sprawling house in Avondale. I think I can sum up what this holiday was like, just by describing what happened to me on the first day. Phil picked me up at the airport and I was absolutely thrilled to see him and all his friends.

We went back to his house and he showed me my room. I had a quick shower and got changed. It was coming up to about 11 o'clock in the morning and the sun was beating down. "What would you like to do next", asked Phil. I said, "That's a stupid question, isn't it?" He said, "OK, let's go to the boozer." We jumped into Phil's ancient metallic blue Mini Minor, with a slightly tuned engine and a sports steering wheel. It had white-wall tyres and chrome wheels.

He drove me to the outskirts of town and we headed off on a dusty road towards Lake Mac. It was the dry season and the water in the lake was quite low. We found a remote hotel on the shore of the lake where we were the only customers on this hot afternoon. The waiter came out and asked us what we wanted to drink.

With relish, I announced my order for the first time in six years: "Two Lion lagers please". "Alright", said the waiter and came back with two ice cold beers.

Our plan originally was to have a couple of drinks and then probably go off for lunch somewhere. Unfortunately, or fortunately (depending on which way you look at it), we still found ourselves sitting in the same chairs four hours later, with at least 12 empty bottles of beer scattered around the table.

Needless to say, we never got any lunch that day and it was quite an interesting drive home, with Phil having to put one hand over his eyeball, to stop him seeing double, while he was driving his Mini. This was very reminiscent of what Muffballs used to do when we were driving around in the middle of the night in Karoi, completely steaming, after a session in the local cinema.

The rest of my holiday in Zimbabwe, more or less, was along the same lines as that particular afternoon's activities. We had lots of parties and caught up with all our lost friends that we hadn't seen for years. Even Sparrowfart was available, not to mention Muffballs as well. One of the main attractions of course, was Phil's beautiful sister, Helen, who I must admit; we all had a deep crush on when we were school boys. Helen had grown up into a stunning young doctor. Not only was she beautiful, she was intelligent as well. I remember on my last night in Zimbabwe going to Phil's all-night party prior to my flight on Sunday and having a really long chat with Helen, catching up on all the things that

Caught in a Flap!

I would have loved to talk to her about when we were younger.

Sadly, the next morning I had to return to London, complete with a filthy hangover, but lovely memories of coming back to my old home. Several other trips to Harare followed and usually I went on my own, but towards 1986 things started to change and I would take a female companion with me. Amongst these of course was Debbie, the nurse that I met on qualifying and of course my wife Ursula, who came with me in the early nineties.

However, there was one visit that sticks in my mind and that was my first holiday with a female companion, who wasn't actually my girlfriend at the time. My little girls are quite interested in the story because they know who Lisa is. I met Lisa at Heathwood Hospital and I'm sure that there should be a whole chapter about Heathwood Hospital lurking somewhere in this book. Lisa is still a good friend of mine and I introduced her to my other handsome friend from London, who was called 'Pretty Boy Phil'. I won't get bogged down with a 'Pretty Boy Phil' story just yet, but I will mention him at some point. Lisa was a young doctor who was doing her senior house officer attachment in obstetrics and gynaecology where I was the resident registrar. Those days were absolutely marvellous for two reasons.

First of all, the hospital was really lovely to work in and secondly, the grounds and accommodation in that lovely part of the world near Ascot race course were idyllic. We had beautiful en-suite bedrooms overlooking our own swimming pool, not to mention the doctors' mess, which was like a whole house for us to go to at the end of a long day. We all lived together and none of us really had a flat or other accommodation, so it was like a community of young people all enjoying themselves together. The consultants were very pleasant, the midwives were really helpful, and most importantly of all, it was very friendly and there was a lovely lady called Pat who managed the general office.

Pat used to ask me to fill in the cremation forms when people had died and this is a rather amusing point for me to remember, because this is how I met my future wife. Two people had to sign the crematorium form to make sure that nothing suspicious had happened to the person before they had died. My job, as a reasonably senior doctor, was to sign the second part of the form having checked the notes and seen that the first part had been completed properly. The first part of the form was usually signed by a very junior doctor called a house officer. Ursula Wolfe was such a doctor on call one night when a patient had died. She was a young visiting German and had blonde crimped hair.

She was very quietly spoken and loved cooking. She wore fashionable glasses, which partially concealed the fact that one eyeball was slightly bigger than the other. I was asked to come and sign the cremation form after Ursula had completed the part one. I started to look through the notes to see what had happened to this poor patient and to make sure there were no suspicious circumstances. Ursula had written in her beautiful handwriting in crystal clear English the following sentence; 'By the time I arrived the patient was dead already'. I burst into a fit of laughter in Pat's office and then phoned Dr Wolfe and said to her, "I am sorry to hear that the patient couldn't wait for you to arrive!" Needless to say Ursula, in her German way, did not appreciate my humour. That is how we met.

Going back to Lisa, the top class student from a Leicester University, she was one of the most conscientious and surefooted women I'd ever met. She was absolutely meticulous about her work and knew exactly what she wanted. She was quite an impressive figure of a woman, being tall with a statuesque swimmer's physique. She was indeed a very good swimmer. She had lovely long legs, long brown hair and a really engaging smile.

I liked working with Lisa, because she worked hard, was conscientious and knew her stuff. She was never ever lazy. I met Lisa at a rather unfortunate time of my life. My girlfriend at the time (who I was quite enraptured with) had completely and unexpectedly dumped me one Monday evening, in the late summer of 1991. The story of this girl may well feature in any future memoirs, but suffice to say Lisa was acutely aware that I was rather upset. Interestingly enough, Lisa had also recently experienced a similar mishap, with a boyfriend who had done a runner.

We both, therefore, found ourselves in similar predicaments and in an effort to cheer ourselves up, I hinted that she may wish to come to Africa with me, to see all the animals and go down the rapids on the Zambezi River at Victoria Falls. Lisa was thrilled with this idea and if I remember correctly, it wasn't me who had specifically suggested this trip. I think it was her idea because she had asked me what Africa was like and I had told her how many times I'd gone back to see my friends. I think it's true to say that she really wanted to go.

Its funny how flippant remarks like, "I'll show you Africa if you want me to", can turn into a major holiday experience. This was the first holiday that I had arranged with a companion that wasn't my girlfriend. We had to book the tickets quite a long way in advance and interestingly, over the following six weeks, I introduced Lisa to 'Pretty Boy Phil' and in no time they were dating. My relationship with Ursula developed into a much stronger friendship and eventually we became two couples. This left us all in a rather unusual situation because Lisa and I had no intention of cancelling our holiday and understandably, Phil was a bit apprehensive about her going on holiday with another man. Ursula, in her usual easy going way, didn't seem too put out.

I offered my usual assurances to all parties concerned, that no hanky panky would be occurring and Lisa made quite sure that I was clear in my mind where we stood.

The holiday therefore went ahead. We flew out on a Friday night and arrived on the usual Saturday morning to be welcomed by my close friend Phil. Phil had now changed his mess and moved into a magnificent house in the suburbs of Highlands in Harare. This grand, five-bedroom sprawling house had a magnificent red tin roof. During the rainy season, the noise was absolutely resounding and incredibly soporific at night, especially when you'd had a few too many Lion lagers.

The grounds were all slightly neglected, with a tennis court that seemed to be vanishing under the weeds, not to mention the empty swimming pool. However it was still very appealing, with the beautiful array of flowers in different colours, not to mention the thick green grass with a backdrop of deep red African soil in the flowerbeds. He had a lovely lolloping dog called Duke, who used to try and eat piri piri chicken leftovers without burning his mouth. He used to slobber all over them so franticly, that the saliva would dilute the hot sauce and then he'd eventually be able to chew it. This was quite a hysterical thing to watch and I still think that he really enjoyed the flavour.

Lisa was quite taken aback by the slightly unkempt way the house was looked after, but soon grew to realise that this was a typical bachelor paradise, with four men living in a house and two servants looking after them. Unfortunately, Phil had misinterpreted my intentions with Lisa and put us both in the same bedroom. This obviously made things a bit difficult, so I decided that the honourable thing to do would be to book into a hotel. Before making the appropriate inquiries however, I went through my usual ritual of having a shower after the ten-hour flight from London. This is where the thrust of my story begins. I went into Phil's bathroom and remember vividly that after having had my shower, the towel that I picked up was damp.

The bathroom was shared by all the individuals in the house. I dried myself with somebody else's towel! This was because I was too bloody lazy to open my suitcase and pull out a fresh one! This was the beginning of my eventual undoing during this intrepid holiday. I booked a room at the Red Fox Hotel, which was literally around the corner from Phil's house, but Lisa, very charitably told me that it was silly staying in separate rooms in the hotel when all we had to do was to behave ourselves! I thought this was most noble of her and would save me quite a lot of money. We went back to Phil's place and shared his double bed and when we went to other hotels, the same arrangement was in place. None of my friends, my brothers, or my dad believed me when I say that no physical contact took place and the fact that this is true makes my story even more incredible.

The highlight of the holiday was a trip to Victoria Falls. I generously organised flight excursions all over the country so we didn't have to drive anywhere. Before going to Victoria Falls, we spent a few nights at a beautiful location called Tiger Bay, which is on the Kariba peninsula. Tiger Bay was a lovely resort, where all the cabins had thatched roofs but no walls. In other words they were like tents, with all the proper facilities, including a shower and toilet, but no surrounding walls where the bedroom area was. This meant that you could lie in your bed at night looking out over the lake down to the shoreline with absolutely nothing surrounding you and only a thatched roof above your head.

The dining area and main reception had a similar configuration and the whole resort had an airy and spacious feel about it. The downside was that there was absolutely no protection whatsoever against wild animals. It wasn't unusual to wake up in the morning and see a hippopotamus standing a few feet away from the end of your bed. At night you could see the yellow eyes of the crocodiles popping up and down above the tranquil surface of the lake water. Needless to say, it was a nerve racking experience going to sleep on the first night, but one got used to it very quickly.

After Tiger Bay, we moved on to Victoria Falls. I have been a regular visitor to Victoria Falls since 1969 and it never ceases to amaze me. The most impressive thing about it is walking through the forest to get to the gorge and then suddenly hearing this incredible noise of thunderous mountains of falling water. This, in conjunction with the massive mist and steam cloud that envelopes the whole area during the rainy season, makes a magnificent impression.

I never tire of watching the millions and millions of gallons of water hurtling down the rock face into that deep gorge. Lisa was really impressed by the spectacle but couldn't help noticing that the river at the bottom of the gorge had tiny little rafts with people hanging on frantically. This was the white water rafting territory of Africa.

The rapids on the Zambezi are rated as some of the most dangerous and deepest in the world. Predictably Lisa wanted to have a go! We stayed in the Victoria Falls Hotel which has to be one of the best colonial buildings in the world. It is set in a breath-taking location and is a beautiful white-walled building with a huge terrace overlooking the Falls. Magnificent tall reception rooms, with rotating fans on the ceilings and immaculately-dressed waiters complete with white gloves, adorn the whole establishment. There was an air of grace and opulence as well as colonialism that could only be matched by the most prestigious hotels during the Raj days of India.

We had a candlelit dinner in a beautiful dining room where a man played on a grand piano, only to be drowned out completely by the harsh croaking noise of the copulating bullfrogs that filled the pond in front of the hotel entrance. We retired to bed quite early that evening after an exhausting day. The start time for the white—water rafting was incredibly early and I was already getting rather apprehensive, so slept very badly. I had experienced white-water rafting the year before when I had been visiting Phil and Muffballs. It was a pretty terrifying experience then, particularly as

Caught in a Flap!

I was on tour with a group of incredibly drunk farmers from Karoi.

My apprehension lifted a little bit, when I saw that our guide looked like a very competent American man, who was in his late twenties. He was of tall stature, had a good physique and looked strong enough to control one of these rafts. The trouble was, it was obvious to me that he had taken a shine to Lisa and I think he was rather keen to show off, or certainly show me up. We went through the usual safety ritual, where he was explaining to us how we should move around the raft and how we should leap to the left or right and to the front or back depending on what rapids we were encountering.

It also depended on how deep they were, which way the wind was blowing, how big the waves were and so on and so forth.

He was clearly enjoying the role as team leader. "Fling to the left", he shouted, "Fling to the right, fling forwards, and fling backwards!" We were all practising to balance the boat for unfavourable conditions whilst waiting in the quiet estuary, for about twenty minutes.

I could not help noticing a large, traditionally-dressed Indian family with children in the next raft all looking unhappy. Apparently, they thought that they had booked the pleasure boat trip (with afternoon tea), on the tranquil part of the river above the Falls!

The great thing about white-water rafting is the fact that it creeps up on you from behind. The first twenty minutes puts you in a state of false security, as you glide beautifully down tranquil waters without any hint of danger. You feel quite cosy in your large Avon inflatable raft, with a guide to take you. How things change dramatically when you go round that next corner! All of a sudden, whilst you are quietly paddling, a rustling noise starts to encroach upon your consciousness. This rustling noise suddenly gets louder as you go round the corner by some huge baobab trees with boulders near them. The rustling noise gets deafening as you approach the horizon, which suddenly vanishes! Then you realise that the water is about to drop away literally from under your feet.

Going over that rapid is the most frightening experience I have ever had. Just imagine sitting in a raft on top of a two-storey house and being pushed over the edge. The experience is totally terrifying as you go hurtling in an almost vertical direction towards the uncompromising depths of angry water below. The raft and all its occupants hurtle down at an alarming speed and almost invariably everyone is flung out into the swirling waters. Miraculously, on this occasion, despite all our screaming, we all stayed inside our boat and managed to land in an upright position after our horrendous drop. The rest of the day was far less traumatic, because the other rapids weren't as frightening.

It's true to say that it is a tremendously exhausting experience and it doesn't help when the chap in charge of the raft is showing off in front of your female companion. I made the fatal mistake of moving around the boat without asking him. I got a terrible rebuke for not holding on tightly and adopting the correct posture when we were about to hit another wave. I felt very embarrassed.

That evening, when we were all in the local bar watching the videos of our adventure, I was sorely tempted to go and say something unpleasant to this lanky American who really fancied himself, but unfortunately, the words just would not come. I remember he had quite marked varicosities of his leg veins and I was hoping that he was crippled by bad haemorrhoids as well! In any event, Lisa had a marvellous day as well as a really good holiday with me. One thing I can remember through this entire vacation was the feeling of being decidedly unwell some three or four days into the holiday.

On one particular occasion, when we were driving up to the farm in Karoi see Muffballs and his family, I had terrible diarrhoea and a feeling of incredible nausea not to mention a fever. I felt truly under the weather. When I eventually arrived, I was certainly in no condition to do my usual three to four hours of continuous after dinner speaking where I entertained all the local farmers as well as Muff's brothers and their wives.

On a previous occasion, some two years before, I was able to talk continuously about all the experiences that I have had in the world of medicine and about being a junior doctor. A little bit like writing this book actually. I remember telling the story about Mr Reynolds' bag and all the Rhodesian farmers were falling about laughing, whilst we downed gallons of lagers and Castle Pilsners.

Caught in a Flap!

On this occasion however, I felt so under the weather that one of my usual fans called Ashley, who was married to Muff's brother, said I was a bit pathetic and off form with my story-telling. Little did she realise how awful I felt and how I just wanted to curl up in a corner and quietly pass away. The cause of all this mishap was soon to become apparent.

We left Zimbabwe on a Sunday night, making the disastrous mistake of going directly to work from the airport the next morning! Whilst waiting in the departure lounge, I was pondering why my eczema was playing me up so much. Instead of being itchy all over my face and around my eyebrows, I couldn't understand why it was extremely itchy in my genital area!

Why would the eczema go down to my pubic hair, I thought? Why was I so uncomfortable down there and why did it itch so much? I decided that the best thing to do was to apply some of the steroid cream that I usually put on my face, to the affected area in an effort to make the situation a little more bearable. Fortunately, I had some cream with me and I retired to the men's lavatory to do the appropriate application.

All throughout the flight I felt awful, tired and more importantly itchy. I got to work the next day, after the ten-hour flight feeling decidedly off colour. I was so poorly that I wasn't even really able to show much enthusiasm about seeing Ursula again. That night I returned to my funny little flat that I shared with the airline hostesses and went to bed early, feeling decidedly miserable. The next morning I woke up and went to the bathroom to do my usual ablutions. I sat on the lavatory, still quizzical about why I was so itchy down below.

I picked up a little flake of skin whilst I was scratching my nether regions and inspected it by putting it on the tiled shelf adjacent to the sink. To my amazement, this little flake of skin started to run off all by itself! "Oh my God", I thought, "I've got some horrible parasitic disease!" Then it suddenly dawned on me . . . the wet towel, the strange room in the cheap hotel, the grubby lavatory seats in the night club in Harare and so on and so forth. "Oh God", I thought, "I've got crabs!"

Have you ever tried telling your girlfriend, who was a little bit worried about you going away with a strange woman that you've come back with crabs, which you have been treating with steroid cream? If these crabs were anything like athletes taking steroids they would be Olympians! I had been feeding and bolstering them up to such an extent that they could probably take over the universe! I was truly embarrassed. The situation became worse when I went to work the next day. I asked a rather non-discrete pharmacist for treatment for my tiny African companions! He very bemusedly gave me a bottle of lotion (which I had to shampoo with) and of course a bottle for my partner Ursula. Later on that morning the whole hospital knew of my plight!

I still have not been able to convince anybody in my circle of friends, or in my family, that I must be the only person in the world who could get a dose of super athletic steroid-popping pubic lice, without even touching a woman!

Chapter 25
The Freshly Laundered Cock

Throughout my professional life, I've come into contact with literally hundreds of individuals who have been having traumatic relationships, bust-ups with their partners, divorces and general unhappiness. Most of these contacts are generally with patients in the clinic, who explain to me that one of the reasons they're feeling depressed and more fed up than normal with their gynaecological problems is because they are going through difficulties with their relationship. In the antenatal clinic particularly, I meet many heavily pregnant women whose partners are fed up with the pregnancy and have expressed fleeting ideas about seeking slim, nubile young women elsewhere.

On the gynaecology front I often see patients with undiagnosed pelvic and abdominal pains. Many of these younger women transpire to having difficulties in their relationships or marriages, when put under closer questioning. This is not to imply that there is something fundamentally wrong with these women, it's just that being in constant contact with them on a day-to-day basis allows me to hear a lot about their unhappy state of affairs with regards to the opposite sex. Sometimes men are so cruel! However, besides this rather sad aspect of relationships, there has always been, to my mind, a hilarious side to it as well.

The hilarious side I refer to relates to how men behave themselves when relationship disasters occur and the 'boot is on the other foot'. I think it is fair to say that women are far more resilient and stronger in themselves when it comes to breaking up with a partner, particularly in the 'Dear John' letter type of scenario. In fact, I think the 'Dear John' letter writers are probably the most ruthless type of women that I have ever encountered.

Women seem to have a self protecting mechanism which makes sure that they will outlive us men. I can realistically see a day in the future of mankind, where men will no longer be required, even for the purpose of reproduction! God knows they can already grow cysts on their ovaries, which contain teeth, hair, skin, brain and bone, without even having had intercourse!

Des Parunia

This story is all about a disillusioned young man, who lived in Africa and couldn't understand why he could not hold down a long-term relationship. I once again refer back to the marvellous days in Africa, when I used to be a footloose and fancy-free young man. All I worried about was my 'A' level results and the possibility of getting into medical school. Looking back, in fact, that was quite a lot of worry and my friend Phil, who I've told you about already, was also under a lot of pressure with his electrical engineering degree.

Having both struggled with our 'A' levels and through university, Phil and I found ourselves in two completely different environments. Phil, after his very successful first-class honours degree in electrical engineering was living in a mess whilst I was in London studying medicine.

As I have mentioned before, a 'mess' is, in Rhodesian terms, a rather nice house, say in a pleasant leafy suburb of Salisbury, where there are at least four or even five rooms available for young men to all live together under the same roof. On the face of it, it sounds like paradise. There are no women there to tell you what to do or when to wash up. In fact you don't have to wash if you don't want to. The added bonus of having servants means that everything is done for you, including your washing, ironing and cooking. There is even someone to polish your shoes.

For a young bachelor with a reasonable salary, it cannot get much better than this! Whilst Phil was living in his mess, I was experiencing a different kind of paradise in the Moullin Memorial Hostel, living with the beautiful ballet dancers and having marvellous exploits, which I have already mentioned.

Phil's life however, was completely different. He could literally do whatever he liked, without the worry of a warden knocking on his door at 11 o'clock at night asking, "Is there anybody in there and if there is, would you ask her to go back to her room?" One of Phil's most notorious inmates was a chap called Bruce, who by all accounts, was quite 'rough and ready'. Now Phil tells me loads of stories about life in his terrific mess environment and I have also witnessed it myself.

During my visits to Harare after I had qualified, I would always stay in one of the rooms in the mess. In fact, it was one of those stays in Phil's mess that left me with the unenviable problem of 'crab lice on steroids,' which I have mentioned previously.

One of the features of this mess way of life was the amazing willingness of the inmates to actually share girlfriends! It was not uncommon, for example, to date one girl for a few weeks and then find out that she was in the other chap's bedroom having a good time, only to come back to you a few weeks later, if the other chap happened to be away or out of town! This amazing freedom of passing girls from one man to another and men being passed from one girl to another, seemed to be a normal part of the Rhodesian way of life in the early eighties.

Bruce, on the other hand, had a slightly more complex problem. He couldn't understand why girlfriends didn't last for very long under his courtship. He was obviously very nice to them and knew how to 'wine and dine' them. By all accounts he seemed to be perfectly acceptable in the 'bedroom performance' category, but for some strange reason, the relationships hardly ever used to last for more than a few weeks, according to Phil.

Phil and I found ourselves discussing this particular situation in yet another mess environment, but this time, many years later in the mid-nineties somewhere out in Avondale.

The friend that we were staying with happened to be one of Phil's close ex-mess mates and suffice to say' it wasn't too surprising to find out that Phil and he had been sharing the same girlfriend, when they had been in a mess together some five or so years earlier!

So, ironic is it not, that Phil ended up marrying this girl and went out to New Zealand to start a new life. Then, Phil's mess mate came over to New Zealand to see how they were all getting on. You can guess the rest. The two of them went out for a date together leaving Phil at home to look after the children! Funny how things never change!

By the pool, that sunny afternoon in Avondale, we three lads found ourselves talking about the marvellous exploits in Phil's mess during those glorious days of the early eighties. We were talking about why Bruce found it so difficult to hold down a relationship and then Phil suddenly came up with his marvellous theory.

On reflection, I'm sure this was absolutely hitting the spot. Bruce's problem was his bedroom etiquette.

Phil took a deep breath and a huge swig of Lion Lager as his feet dangled casually in the swimming pool. He went on to tell us that Bruce was quite a good-looking, rugged (albeit a little bit scruffy) 'Rhodesian type', hunky sort of bloke.

He had a reasonable job in town and spent a lot of time playing sport. He also had an amazing track record of loads of girlfriends that all seemed to clear off rather quickly, for some inexplicable reason. It definitely wasn't halitosis. It certainly wasn't his personality per se and it wasn't because he was a 'Rhodesian male chauvinist pig'. In fact it was a bit of a mystery why this attractive male couldn't keep his girls.

The situation would have been understandable if he was looking for a huge variety in his life and was quite happy about the girls moving on to another boyfriend, so that he could try new ones, but that was not the case. Phil's explanation was quite simple and based solely on what Bruce told Phil about his usual routine in the bedroom. Phil continued his narrative. "Well you see boys", he said, "Bruce had a certain thing about sex."

We all looked inquisitively at Phil as he continued with his sentence. Our imaginations were running wild thinking about all sorts of evil, demonic, sexual perversity and so forth. Activity bad enough to put any young women off ever coming back to the Avondale mess. It was much simpler than that. Bruce's problem was quite straightforward. Phil told us with relish how, on a typical Saturday or Sunday afternoon, Bruce would bring one of the beautiful young girls up to his bedroom and make love to her all afternoon. This was usually after a good session down at the local Reps Theatre bar, or at some other equally boozy venue such as a sports club or the George Hotel.

Bruce's fatal mistake, after offering his charms to these girls, was beautifully described by Phil. We all knew there was a big climax coming up and Phil told us. "After he'd made love to one of these chicks, Bruce, when he'd decided that he had completely finished, would leap out of bed, prance into the bathroom and rush up to the sink, where he would ferociously scrub and wash his entire genital region, including his ring piece! After generously sprinkling his wedding tackle with fragrant talcum powder, he would then casually ponce back to the boudoir and then lie on the bed next to the girl, with his freshly-laundered cock nonchalantly draped across his thigh!"

Phil has told me this story at least a hundred times and I keep asking him to do it again just to hear the punch line: "The guy is having steaming sex with this girl all afternoon and then he just vanishes and comes back displaying his freshly laundered cock, while she's lying there all steamy and sticky. It's hardly surprising that the girls used to 'pull a fade' after that!"

I still think this is Phil's most hilarious story and till his dying day I will always remember him for telling it to me. The catchphrase 'freshly laundered cock' is unique to Phil's narrative and to my mind, has never been described in any other romantic situation anywhere else in the world.

Chapter 26
Dream On

My Ascot days, as a relatively young man with a new Alfa Romeo Spider, were really quite jolly considering the turmoil that I was going through at the time. I had found myself homeless after splitting up with the lovely Debbie. It is hard to believe that we had bought a flat together, followed by a major separation and selling of the property and then found ourselves back together again, only to buy another property, this time in the form of a terraced house. Those turbulent times were all spent in Chiswick. It is incredible that we split up yet again and I found myself living in rented accommodation somewhere in Northfields, West London.

The plus side of this generally unhappy time was the fact that I was sharing the flat with no less than four young air hostesses. I used to spend most of my off-duty time living in the flat with the girls. However, on occasions the attraction of Ascot, particularly in the summer, often left me using my on-call accommodation, especially when there were attractive young women floating about the hospital! I remember one pleasant afternoon returning from a wedding in Taunton.

I had attended this wedding with one of my Charing Cross nursing friends called Pamela and having dropped her off at the station, I found myself languishing in my on-call room on a lovely warm Sunday afternoon. There had been a particularly attractive young woman called Astrid, whom I'd had my eye on for some time. She was exquisitely unobtainable and I believe already had a boyfriend.

Having said that, it was always a pleasure to watch her doing the ward rounds. She had an amazing ability to flirt in such a delightful way and her other appeal was a deliciously addictive and mischievous giggle.

I kept bumping into Astrid on the ward rounds as our paths crossed from one department to another. I never had the nerve to even think about asking her out, so it came as quite an enormous surprise on that Sunday afternoon, while I lay in my hospital accommodation contemplating what to do next, that I got a phone call from her. Astrid was on call and had seen my little red sports car in the hospital grounds. She very amicably asked if she could come up to my room and have a chat. I could not believe my luck! To cut a long story short, she came up and spent no less than three hours talking to me.

I don't think that I even made her a cup of coffee. She sat crossed legged on my bed and we talked about absolutely everything. Then as quickly as she arrived, she vanished, back to the hospital to attend her duties. I remember bumping into her the next day as if nothing had happened. It took me ages to pluck up the courage to formally ask her out, several weeks later.

The other joy of being a junior doctor at Ascot, besides of course these unexpected liaisons with beautiful women, was the camaraderie that I experienced during those lovely times in our junior doctors' mess. The junior doctor's mess nowadays is probably a relic of the past. Hardly any proper messes exist now and the concept of a group of young doctors having a few beers and a curry, when they were all on duty together, has now really died a death.

Hospital parties are a thing of the past and the glorious Christmas times, when the different departments would have separate parties during the four weeks before Christmas Day, certainly do not exist any more, because of the legislation about alcohol on hospital premises and so on and so forth.

Our doctors' mess at Ascot was a semi-detached house complete with a kitchen and large dining/lounge areas. Upstairs there were several small bedrooms. This was of course; completely separate from our other main hospital lodgings, such as detached married accommodation, as well as the marvellous converted old country house with its swimming pool outside in the back garden. Barbeque and swimming pool parties were the norm and as winter approached, we often used to have cosy Sunday lunches together in our doctors' mess accommodation.

We had a marvellous team leader in the form of the mess chairman called Alan. This cuddly, jovial Northerner would regularly organise wine and champagne tasting evenings, often during the week. On one particular occasion, my dad came to join me for one of these evenings, as he was attending a conference somewhere in London and was due to present a paper the next day. The wine and champagne tasting went on for about three hours in the mess and then we all decided to go down to the local Tandoori and have a slap-up curry.

What a great boozy evening! Quite a few people were sick, because of over indulgence and my mother was shocked to see my dad return from the conference the following day, with a huge blob of tikka masala mixed with tarka dall and Rogan josh all down the back of his tweed jacket! I can't believe that he presented a paper without anybody noticing the contents of half the local curry house scattered across his back!

There were some really funny characters in that doctors' mess whom I had the pleasure of meeting over my two year attachment as a junior registrar. However, there is one specific individual who has left an indelible mark on my mind, regarding the typical male view on the female sexual response.

This memory comes from a particularly ordinary afternoon, sometime during the middle of the week, when we had all gathered together for our usual lunch break. For some strange reason, my antenatal clinic had finished earlier than expected and I found myself wandering over to the doctors' mess dining room, attracted to a rather nice smell of pasta and garlic coming from the kitchen. Young Ursula of 'when I arrived he was dead already' fame, was doing her usual trick of making everyone lunch. Gathered round the dining room table were three of the newly-recruited young house officers.

They were particularly attractive and showed a wide variety in shape and size. There was a plump blonde who looked very cuddly.

There was a tall, slim girl with long dark hair, who looked as if she could do a stint on the catwalks and the third one was somewhere in between. She had a rather intellectual looking expression and wide-framed glasses. These girls were all rather lovely in their own right and appeared to be deeply engrossed in a magazine article that they were sharing.

The article was from 'Cosmopolitan' and was addressing the importance of the newly highly publicised concept of the female G-spot. I was quietly observing the spectacle from the other end of the dining room table.

The girls avidly read the article together and made occasional comments as they did so. The short plump one was expressing how refreshing it was that men were becoming aware of the concept of the G-spot and its importance.

The tall, thin girl was quizzical about how many men would actually be bothered to take the time and stimulate this particular part of the female anatomy during the course of routine love-making. The third girl was quite adamant that most sympathetic and well educated men would take the trouble to find out where the G-spot was and give the woman the maximum amount of pleasure.

I found the whole dialogue very intriguing. The girls carried on reading and gesticulating about the contents of the article. The tall one again described out loud how the G-spot was a remnant of the male prostate and she was aware of some men enjoying their prostate being massaged during intercourse. I found all of this a little bit overpowering, I must say. Anyway, I tried to quash my prudishness and continued to listen to their conversation. The intellectual girl concluded, after they had finished the last paragraph of the article, that how brilliant it was that men nowadays were so well educated and generally speaking, so much more skilful in bed than their counterparts from years ago. I could not help sniggering quietly on listening to this revelation about young British men!

At this point, one of the girls noticed me sitting at the end of the table obviously engrossed in their conversation. "What do you think about what we are saying?" she asked. I pretended to be distracted and not really au-fait with their previous conversation. "What do you mean exactly?" I asked back, "I was only sort of half listening to what you were saying". "Well" she said, "This article states that young British men have become more familiar with the concept of the G-spot as a result of being generally better educated. It states that they have become more considerate in the bedroom and more conscious of the female's sexual desires and wishes.

We think that it is probably true and think they have become more considerate. "What do you think Mikey?" I fumbled for an answer, not wishing to expose my general lack of knowledge on this subject, bearing in mind that most of what I'd listened to was completely new to me! I had a sudden wave of inspirational genius. "I know", I said, "Why don't you ask the next young man who walks into this dining room what he thinks about the G-spot? There is after all only one door in and one door out, which gives him approximately five seconds to answer", I said rather cheekily. "OK then", said Vanessa, the tall one, "we will wait for the next bloke to walk through."

I could not have chosen a better candidate for the job. Within a few seconds a tall, good looking young house officer, complete with a pony tail arrived at the front door of our dining room. Not only was he trendy and well educated, but he was also artistic and played the guitar in a local band. He had a slightly casual demeanour about him and I remember being quite shocked that he did not wear a tie for work! He strutted into the dining room, complete with his white coat, neatly ironed Levi jeans and a white cheesecloth shirt. "Hey Davy", gushed Vanessa in a slightly excited voice, "What do you think of the G-spot?" Davy continued walking and looked completely unperturbed.

He then looked deeply into Vanessa's eyes and said, "As long as I come, who gives a fuck!" He then vanished through the other door of the dining room within about one second. The three girls looked at each other, all with their mouths gaping wide open. I sniggered quietly and thought to myself, 'Dream on!' The G-spot was never mentioned again during our pasta lunch.

Some time later, I felt extraordinarily tired after the heavy on-call weekend that I had just done. I knew the clinic wasn't going to start for at least half an hour, so I decided to have a little nap in my on-call room overlooking the swimming pool. I lay down on my bed and contemplated the G-spot conversation.

All of a sudden, the phone rang and a pleasant welcoming voice, which I was so familiar with, simply said "Hello" in a rather dulcet tone. "Thank God it's you", I said, "Get yourself up here to the on-call room and make sure that your knickers are off before you get to the top of the stairs." I was exuberant at hearing my girlfriend's voice.

There was quite a long silence, which surprised me a bit and then a deep drawing of breath. "Well, that's very friendly", she said, "It's Miss Rivers and I was wondering whether we could do a ward round before the clinic?"

Miss Rivers was a young, attractive, petite and refined consultant. I had no idea how I could possibly get out of this one, as I nervously ambled my way to the maternity unit!

Chapter 27
The Teenage Colposcopy Cold Coagulation Massacre

It was another long Friday afternoon, doing a colposcopy clinic with devoted colleague Sister Lindy. We always felt that we were the only two people left in the hospital working on a Friday afternoon and today was no exception, during a hot summery mid-August. The clinic had been quite tedious and it was overbooked and Lindy and I were taking a short tea break. I was trying to cheer her up by telling her one of my favourite colposcopy stories from way back, when I was a senior registrar in Surrey.

This particular memoir involved someone I was especially fond of. The man in question had played a very important part through my informative years as a junior doctor and more importantly' had given me a really good solid training in the specialty of obstetrics and gynaecology. Pinky (Pendleton) was a delightful friendly South African with a very mysterious background. He had found himself in England as a middle-grade doctor and I had the pleasure of meeting him shortly after he had imported himself from Cape Town. I was a senior house officer at the time and Pinky was a registrar.

He trained me for at least two years at SHO level and when I was fortunate enough to obtain a registrar post later on in my career, guess who was my senior registrar? Pinky, therefore also trained me as a registrar. To make life even more interesting, later on after I had finished my thesis and obtained a senior registrar position, guess who my consultant was?

This amazing situation allowed me to have most of my training in the hands of one really good friend, as well as a colleague. It was great to always have a boss with such a good sense of humour. He had a marvellous ability to teach and more importantly than all of this, the confidence to let me get on with things without interfering. He was also very generous and at Christmas time he would always give me a nice bonus to buy a present with. At the Christmas parties he would often be quite boisterous.

I remember on one occasion, when I arrived with my brother during the fateful night of the 'all talk and no trousers' experience, Pinky was so happy to see me that he rugby tackled me in front of a huge table of food. This caused me to fall over and vanish underneath the table, only to emerge on the other side covered in Jamaican patties and the contents of a carafe of rum punch!

Much of my education was in sharing pints, either after work or on call, in the cosy pub called 'The Cat'. It's funny how much you can learn from talking to somebody over a pint! Gone are the days when you could do a nice Friday afternoon ward round at the local pub with all your juniors. How times have changed!

Anyway, getting back to the funny story to try and cheer up Lindy. It was a cold winter's afternoon and I remember relishing my new purchase of a Rolex Oyster watch, which I'd acquired from one of the wealthy vascular surgeons. His son had not wanted it for his 21st birthday present and the father was keen to sell it. I had been offered this watch to celebrate my 40th birthday and I got it for a bargain basement price. Naturally I was quite thrilled with myself! I was looking forward to showing it to my boss Pinky later on that afternoon.

Pinky was a bit late for the colposcopy clinic, because he had gone for his monthly haircut and I believe he'd decided to also treat himself to a new suit from a tailor somewhere in Croydon. He eventually arrived at the clinic just as I was finishing seeing the first patient. I had come out to greet him and he looked spruced up with a neat haircut and a beautiful new dark woollen suit.

The sister in charge of the clinic, a delightful West Indian woman in her late fifties called Sister Flo Jo, acknowledged Mr Pendleton's new appearance by saying, "Lordy, Lordy, what a brilliant suit man. Is it from Perry Cardine?" I felt rather bemused at her interpretation of the name of his suit? "Shit hey", retorted Pinky in his typical rich South African accent. "You have to feel the quality of this cloth to believe it man", he said proudly.

Pinky's first patient of the afternoon was an extremely nervous woman, who had to have a barrage of major tranquillisers in the clinic prior to being seen for her treatment. She had a particularly large lesion on her cervix and Pinky wanted to show me how to do a wide loop excision biopsy of the disease. He needed to use the colposcope to look up into the vagina. He also needed some special apparatus in the form of a cheese wire loop on the end of a handle, which would effortlessly shave off a piece of the affected cervix.

This fine cheese wire was mounted on the end of a pencil-like device with a button to activate the current to facilitate the cutting of the tissues. He also needed a gas extractor and a suction pipe joined up to the examining speculum, so that the smoke created could be sucked out away from the field of view. This entire procedure was going to be done under local anaesthesia in the outpatient setting.

I waited with interest to see how he would tackle this rather challengingly large, nervous patient, whose legs were already trembling before we had even correctly positioned her bottom on the end of the examination couch. She was a rather neurotic headmistress of one of the local primary schools and had recently returned from a school trip to the South of France. Here she had met another estranged headmaster, leading inevitably to a dose of penile virus particles and a subsequent abnormal smear. Hence the trip to the colposcopy clinic!

Pinky skilfully set up all his equipment and explained to the patient how he was going to give her some anaesthesia. He used to call me James, which I thought was amusing, given that I knew him so well. He said brusquely to me, "Listen James, beware of giving large doses of anaesthesia to these patients, because sometimes the needle going into the cervix can cause quite a lot of pain and they can get a real humdinger of a vasovagal attack." I asked him if this was a common occurrence and he responded, "Very rare in my hands." I then asked him what the worst manifestation of a vasovagal attack was.

He again responded confidently by describing that some patients can actually have a cardiac arrest. He said all of this quite quietly, because of the anxious patient. He then went on to whisper, "But sometimes they can have an explosive and completely involuntary bowel movement there and then." How hideously embarrassing, I thought to myself.

Pinky continued his demonstration of how to insert local anaesthesia using a dental syringe needle into the cervix. After the second ampoule, the patient let off a peculiar moaning sound and looked as if she was about to pass out. Pinky promptly withdrew the syringe, only to witness the most encrmous bowel movement that either of us had ever seen in our lives! She had obviously enjoyed the delights of the local Tandoori the night before and she promptly released a bucketful of warm, wet stool all over Pinky's brand new Pierre Cardin suit trousers.

Desperate to try and keep a straight face, I retreated from the area, only to comment to sister outside the treatment room, "My God, that's the biggest bowel movement I have ever seen in Pinky's clinic, sister!" She responded dryly, "Lordy, Lordy, I believe that was nothing compared to what has just come out of 'his' backside!"

Lindy was obviously cheered up by this story and we prepared to see our next patient, not having any idea that we were on the brink of a similar disaster.

Caught in a Flap!

This next patient, unusually in a colposcopy clinic, was a young teenage schoolgirl. I remember that she had a green uniform and was in the upper sixth at grammar school. She was quite a confident young lady and deputy head girl. Nonetheless she needed a colposcopy for an abnormal smear. She was accompanied by a rather nervous-looking mother who was a typical middle class housewife and member of the local school governors' committee. She also worked in an Oxfam charity shop at the weekends. She was wearing a twin set and pearls in keeping with her role of the spouse of the Master of the local Masonic lodge.

The mother insisted on attending her young, blonde daughter's consultation, which made it very tricky for me to extract the appropriate sexual and contraceptive history, so vital in the art of colposcopy! She kept on saying that there were no secrets between her and her daughter and I wondered whether she really knew about the daughter's steamy affair with the school's 34 year old karate teacher!

Needless to say, the mother also wanted to attend the colposcopic examination and make sure that 'Precious Penelope' was alright. I somewhat reluctantly agreed.

In the colposcopy examination room, Penelope found herself lying on the examination couch with her legs up in stirrups with her twitchy mother holding her hand. I performed my usual colposcopy examination and presented Penelope with a good quality colour image up on the television screen joined to my colposcope. Fortunately, there was very little in the way of disease to see on the cervix but there was a very small warty area visible on the lower lip. I explained to my patient what I thought this was and asked for permission to take a small biopsy from this area.

This request triggered the inevitable barrage of tedious questions from the 'twin set and pearls'. "How did she get this? Does it come from boys? Is it contagious? Does it cause cancer?" I skilfully dodged the questions as well as I could by asking for the 'long-reach' biopsy forceps and directing them to my target on the cervix. With a characteristic click, the jaws locked and a neat little cylinder of tissue was removed, along with the usual tiny spurt of blood. Penelope declined to watch, but her mother was riveted with attention.

Unfortunately, I had left my examining microscope on full power and the TV image of the dribbling biopsy site had been scaled up to look more like Victoria Falls! It gave the illusion of a major haemorrhage, so much so in fact that the blood started to drain from the mother's face and she became terribly pale. In the next split second, Lindy noticed the characteristic trickling sound of someone wetting themselves, as the mother fainted and slumped down to the floor.

She was lying in her own puddle and Lindy leapt to her rescue only to slip in the wee and fall back violently towards me. From my stool I ducked down as much as I could, but it was too late. Lindy crashed into the colposcope sending the camera and lens hurtling towards my head on the end of its long robotic arm. Crash!

I was knocked clean to the floor to join the other two ladies in the pool of pee! Meanwhile, Penelope gazed down nonchalantly, casually inspecting her nail varnish as she did so. As the cleaning lady walked in with her bucket and mop, I glanced up towards Penelope and spluttered, "Now why don't you knock the cleaner out and then you will have nailed the 'whole' department?"

Lindy had to give the incontinent mother some bright green theatre trousers to go home in.

They clashed quite badly with the pearls.

Chapter 28
The Story Of The Secretive Goolies

Even as a seasoned gynaecologist after some 12 years in practice as a consultant, I find myself regularly in situations where I can't believe my eyes or ears. There was always something out there that would surprise or shock me, amuse or beguile me, or downright depress me. On this particular occasion, it was a combination of more or less all of these emotions. I was doing my routine labour ward session looking after the delivery suite for the morning. My duties included supervising the registrar and making sure that the SHOs got some training. But most importantly of all, I had to try and get the elective caesarean sections done on time.

Usually there were three elective caesarean sections on a Tuesday. Sometimes, if the delivery suite was particularly busy and we had to do emergency or urgent caesarean sections, the list would get snookered and we would have to carry on into the afternoon. This was not a good thing, because postponement of these operations resulted in upsetting the patients and more importantly the hospital managers, who did not want to incur the added expense of bringing extra theatre staff in for the afternoon. The pressure was obviously always there to get on with the job.

As bad luck would have it on this particular day, all three caesareans were difficult. There was one in question which sticks firmly in my mind. She was an enormously fat lady with three previous caesarean sections, who now found herself pregnant for the fourth time and of course needed another one.

What makes this story particularly interesting is the fact that her fourth caesarean was so difficult for me to do. Not only did I have to plough my way through a mountain of fat just to get to her abdominal wall, but the wall itself was scarred and battered from all the previous surgery. Gaining access to her pelvis was a bit like one of those Indiana quests to find the Ark or the Holy Grail. Her anatomy, at best, was just a mess and at worst, a complete disaster. Just trying to isolate the uterus taxed me to the limit, but eventually I was able to find the uterus, push down the bladder, make the appropriate incision and hopefully deliver infant number four.

However things were just about to get worse, because of all the previous operations that she'd had in her pelvis, the womb was quite scarred and the tissues quite friable. On entering the uterus and making the appropriate enlargement of the incision to enable me to extract the infant, the inevitable tear occurred and there was excessive bleeding around the corner of the incision. The baby was unexpectedly large and this contributed to more trauma of the uterus as the extraction was so difficult. It is safe to say that the whole operation was turning into a 'dog's dinner'. She was bleeding profusely.

The access was difficult and the tissues were of poor quality. The sutures were tearing through the muscle and making the bleeding worse. I was getting quite fed up. We had already reached about one and a half litres of blood loss and I still hadn't properly closed the uterus. The suction machine was working overtime to try and give me some exposure. The student midwife was getting tetchy, as this was her first time scrubbing for a caesarean section and more importantly, the registrar (my first assistant) was getting bored with the blood loss and the slow progress.

Eventually I was able to close the uterus and secure some degree of reasonable blood loss control. At this point, I reflected on the fact that this was the patient's fourth caesarean section and I glanced down at her rather forlorn-looking husband, who was just a wisp of a man compared to his wife. I then said to him, "Look, this has been a very difficult caesarean section. You've got four children already and this new baby is in lovely condition. Would you let me have the opportunity to offer a sterilisation procedure, so we don't find ourselves in this difficult situation again?" He looked at me and in no uncertain terms, shook his head in total disagreement. 'OK,' I thought as I carried on with closing the abdomen.

A few seconds later when loops of bowel were finding their way into where I was trying to sew and repair, more blood loss started to occur, this time from the broad ligament.

I was getting quite pissed off with the operation at this point, what with loops of bowel getting in the way, further bleeding and the general adiposity of this lady making things more difficult. When I had secured some progress and the situation was looking a little bit better,

I turned round to the husband again and said, "Look, this procedure is becoming very taxing and I don't want to be in this situation again. Please would you consider the possibility of a sterilisation before I come out of the abdomen?" Once again his head shook. I looked over the screen to the mother underneath and said, "Listen, this is really important, would you at least consider the possibility of me performing a more permanent form of contraception?" She shook her head.

The operation continued and became even more tedious. At one point, I thought the bladder had been perforated and I had to start exploring around the pelvis to see whether there was a hole. Fortunately there was not. The bowels kept on tumbling into the field of view and there was generalised ooze from across the uterus. The abdominal wall was going to be a nightmare because it was at least eight inches thick. In desperation I asked once more. In fact, I was almost pleading with the husband. "Sir", I said, "please would you consider the possibility of a sterilisation? This operation is becoming a nightmare and I would dread any other surgeon having to come into your wife's abdomen again."

He again looked at me incredulously and despondently and just shook his head. I was now desperate and just about to close the abdomen. I had one last chance. "Please can I ask you why you are so against the idea of a permanent form of contraception such as sterilisation?" His dark beady eyes piercingly looked at me and he said nervously, "I don't want to show my goolies to all these people."

Here, for the first time in the history of medicine, was a situation where a consultant obstetrician was perceived to be offering his patient's partner a 'public vasectomy' in full view of 8 or 9 theatre staff, midwives, medical students and paediatricians! Needless to say, the rest of the day didn't get much better.

Chapter 29
The Clinic From Hell

The purpose of this chapter is to describe a clinic where some of my worst memories of difficult patients were created. In medical parlance we have an expression called the 'albatross patient'. This is a patient who never goes away and just follows you from one hospital to another throughout your career. Or even worse, when you do get established, she just keeps coming back, never leaving sight of the mother ship. Other doctors call patients like this 'heart—sink' patients.

Whenever such a woman walks into the consulting room, your heart sinks to a really low ebb, making you feel that you will never survive the consultation. A feeling of overwhelming dread manifests itself and you just wish that some 'God Almighty' emergency is occurring somewhere else in the hospital, to give you an excuse to leave the consulting room and go and save somebody else's life, including your own! It really does get that bad.

'Heart-sink' patients and 'albatrosses' take many forms. The most common one is the continual whiner who never gets better. The other is the one that gets better with the condition that you are treating, but keeps generating new ailments and problems that you've never heard of before. This is in an attempt to keep up continuous appearances to torture you in your clinic. These sad people never go away and cause perpetual grief right cross the medical profession, including all specialties known to mankind. God only knows how general practitioners have been able to survive such patients.

The fact that GPs have now stopped doing 'on calls' or night duties and restricted their hours to 40 per week on £100,000 salaries, gives me some inclination about how they have dealt with this terrible problem!

I was asked recently by my marvellous clinic sister Lindy if I could put together a dossier of a 'clinic from hell', recording all the worst possible encounters I've ever had over 25 years and imagining that they all turned up on the same day. In real life, if this had happened I wouldn't be writing this book, because I would have committed 'hara-kiri' somewhere in a dark hospital corridor! For the sake of amusement, I relate my top worst cases and imagine that they all turned up on the same day. Ladies and gentleman I give you my clinic from hell.

Case 1—"Say Cheese!"

Lavonia Lane is a 55 year old woman married to an anally retentive train-spotter husband who has recently retired from a scintillating career in accountancy, somewhere in North Yorkshire. She had two grown-up children who both emigrated to New Zealand, probably just to get away from their parents. Lavonia is peculiar and likes to be called Lav!

She has dreadful bleached blonde hair and a Diana Dores' haircut and wishes that she was still acting as a professional drama teacher rather than a bored housewife. Sometime in her distant past she may have had a decent job with RADA somewhere, but now she finds herself totally redundant and able to lavish hours and hours contemplating her itchy vulva and vagina!

To make matters worse, she has dragged her poor husband into the scenario and with his interest in amateur photography has forced him to take pictures of her genitalia, so as to convince the poor sod consultant caring for her, about the best way forward in managing her almost unmanageable condition. Lavonia has the most inexplicable itch and soreness, which has no pattern to it and doesn't resemble anything written in any of the textbooks describing common vulval dermatosis. She's a unique specimen who has developed signs and symptoms that can only be imagined if one was on a mixture of ecstasy and cocaine.

Everything about her presentation was bizarre. The timing of the itchiness and soreness was completely unpredictable, as it had no aggravating or relieving factors and would come on out of the blue. Intercourse was sometimes alright and on other occasions totally impossible. There were days when her vulva felt quite normal and on other days it felt like a bushfire going on between her legs! To make matters worse, clinical examination always revealed absolutely no abnormality. I tried desperately to contain myself from the point of view of my frustration in trying to manage her.

Should I go for the whole 'Full Monty' experience and bring her in for an examination under anaesthesia and sample every bit of vulval, vaginal and perianal skin, in a desperate bid to get a histological diagnosis that might throw some light on her problem, or should I simply write her off as a complete nutcase and ask her to go away with her Polaroid photographs and see the local dermatologist?

I made the fatal mistake of bringing her in for the 'Full Monty'. Vulval mapping, although sounding like quite an exotic medical procedure, simply means anesthetising the patient and allowing you to examine them when they're unconscious and take appropriate skin samples from any areas that you may be worried about. Given Lavonia's bizarre history and complex presentation, I decided to sample as many skin sites as possible.

I imagined myself as being a little rodent creeping up and down her genital tract and taking a little nibble from here and there. This is essentially what vulval mapping is. I decided to leave no stone unturned and sampled every conceivable different area of skin in an effort to make a proper diagnosis.

Lavonia survived the experience quite nicely and made a good day-care postoperative recovery. She went home that evening. The next formidable task was to see her for a follow up. I discreetly arranged a six-week review to give myself some time to recover from the ordeal of the previous original consultation.

Lavonia and her Polaroid camera husband appeared together, both looking intense, a few weeks later. They stared at me as if I was the 'panacea', 'the God of pain relief and 'the God of vulval itchiness' that would suddenly make everything go away.

After greeting them and inviting them to join me in the consulting room, I feverishly looked for the pathology report from my rather overzealous vulval mapping procedure. I was hoping, if there was a God, that there would be some definite dermatological diagnosis, which I could sell to her as the cause for all her trouble. Alas that was not to be. All the skin specimens showed evidence of straightforward chronic inflammation, which is something anybody with itchiness would have. In desperation, I was wondering whether to look at the last page of the histology report describing the final biopsy from the perianal skin around her bottom. Thank God I did!

At last there was something for me to tell her. The perianal skin biopsy showed wart viral changes! 'Hallelujah' I thought, I'm going to be able to give her a diagnosis, which she certainly won't like! Human papilloma virus changes in the skin mean that you have had intercourse, rather than being a virgin all your life. Human papilloma changes in the vaginal, vulval and perianal skin means that you have acquired a sexually-transmitted disease called HPV infection.

HPV infection is the cause of cervical cancer and all the vulval dysplastic disease, which is responsible (if untreated) for leading to malignant change in any part of the lower genital tract. Human papilloma virus is responsible for genital warts, abnormal smears and cancer. Human papilloma virus is a serious clinical entity, so serious in fact, we have developed a vaccine to combat it. This vaccine should be given to young girls before they become sexually active and acquire the virus from the knobs of the male consorts!

I looked at Lavonia and gazed into her intense, beady blue eyes while her husband nervously fidgeted with his latest Nikon camera management manual. "Well, Mrs Lane", I said, "I think I have found a cause for your vulval itch and irritation." "Excellent", she replied, "What have you found?" "I think you have got evidence of wart virus infection", I said succinctly with enormous clarity.

The consultation that followed can only be described as complete hell. She wanted to know every aspect of the transmission of the wart virus and where it came from. Short of having to tell her that her husband's knob had contracted that virus at some time during their lives (even before they met), this was a very difficult idea to get over in a tactful and sensitive manner.

Lavonia insisted that the only partner she'd ever had was her husband Donald and he was very reluctant to describe any other consorts in his rather brief premarital life. Eventually, I just had to spit it out and tell them that the virus had to have been contracted at some time during the sexual lives of the couple whom I was addressing. Lavonia was not amused and insisted that I start the treatment immediately. She wanted to start a full album of follow-up amateur photo documentation of her nether regions, not to mention a further million follow-up clinic visits. I was well and truly trapped!

Case 2—Give Me A Clue

As a very young and inexperienced registrar, I can remember that this woman who had a consultation in my gynaecology clinic made me feel so depressed and demoralised that I thought if the clinic was going to continue like this, I really was not going to make it through to the next day!

Imagine a 17 stone edentulous blob of a hairy woman, reeking of nicotine and tobacco smoke, with the most awful coloured loose—fitting cotton dress, reminiscent of the big top at Billy Smart's circus on Blackheath. If this wasn't depressing enough, my brief for this patient was to address her problem of primary infertility.

This woman had never been pregnant. My first rather uncharitable reaction on just looking at her was, how anybody could find her attractive enough to indulge in the act of satisfactory coital activity, i.e. become aroused, produce an erection and try to insert the erect penis into her body. I was trying to think of all the people that I've met through my life that might be vaguely interested in such a situation, including a sprinkling of friends and relatives who I suspected may fancy larger women. Despite going down that avenue of fantasy I personally couldn't imagine how anybody would really want to do the business with this poor lady, apart from the Benny Hill character in the film 'The Italian Job'.

I conducted the consultation in an orderly and sensible fashion according to all the guidance that we are given regarding infertile couples. I had to ask her about basic things including her past medical history, medication, allergies, general health, smear history, her psyche and so on. Specifically, I had to address the all important subject of the act of sexual intercourse. Now I needed to do this tactfully, because it was quite obvious that this patient was quite sensitive about her general appearance and more importantly, her overwhelming body mass index.

After all she was almost short of breath sitting there talking to me. God knows what she would have been

Caught in a Flap!

like (from the strain on her heart point of view) if she was on the plateau phase of an impending orgasm on a hot steaming summer night! I had no idea what her husband looked like, but I suspected he might have been the usual tiny wiry stick insect-like creature that seems to like to buzz and hover over these gigantic women!

I went through her history and examination very diligently and then started to discuss with her what I realistically thought her chances of conception, pregnancy and childbirth were. The one overriding worry that I had was simply centred on her enormous size. I was truly concerned that she may compromise her health by becoming pregnant. I had to appreciate that her heart and lungs were already struggling under the enormous burden of obesity.

I also had to acknowledge that her chance of successful penetration, as things stood, was very limited. The terrible old joke medical students used to make about really fat, infertile women sprung to mind. While I looked at her 15 chins (enough to make a good size fire escape for most tall buildings in Canary Wharf), I wondered whether it was safe to advise pregnancy at all in this particular clinical situation.

While I was contemplating this, the medical student joke just wouldn't go away from my mind: What do you do with a huge fat woman who is difficult to penetrate? Well the answer is simply to tell the husband to invest in some shaving foam, bring his good lady wife into the bedroom and then ask her to lie down and open her legs. The husband then liberally squirts the shaving foam over the entire vulval and vaginal area and then says, "Mildred, fart and give me a clue."

Eventually, I summoned up the courage of my convictions and told this lady that I truly felt it wasn't in her best interest for me to procure a pathway, which would end up in achieving a pregnancy given her current medical and clinical condition. She expressed her extreme disappointment by looking at me and replying in no uncertain terms. "Mr James, the trouble with you is that you are a fatist!" I looked at her and thought to myself; well I suppose that's better than being called a chauvinist or a racist. She then left my consulting room in a bit of a huff! Sister then brought in the next set of patient notes. I nearly died when I saw who it was!

Lucy Ballbinder was a true 'albatross' patient who had been following me around for years. And guess what? She was quite enormous! In fact, she was almost as big as Mrs Fatist who had just given me a tongue-lashing. Lucy was one of my infertility patients and her progress to date had reminded me once again, why we gynaecologists have a nick name for infertility clinics. We call them 'futility' clinics!

My problem with this patient was with the results of her postcoital tests. A postcoital test is one of the more revolting things gynaecologists have to do. The couple are asked to have sexual intercourse the night before and the woman attends the clinic the next morning having been told not to wash or bath after the act! The poor doctor then passes a speculum up her vagina, examines the cervix and comments on the quality of the slimy mucus within its canal. Are you with me so far? He then passes a 'straw like' syringe into the canal opening and sucks out some of the blob of mucus mixed with seminal fluid.

He then puts this blob onto a slide and examines it under a microscope, hoping to find evidence of viable active sperms. Whilst doing this, it is not uncommon for the doctor to think to himself; 'Why is there all this fuss about men's girlie magazines and Page 3 girls'?

Mrs Ballbinder and her microscopic husband Terry assured me that satisfactory intercourse had taken place the night before. This was their third attempt at a postcoital test, as the two previous examinations had revealed no sperms whatsoever. This was at odds with Terry's apparently normal semen analysis result. As Mrs Ballbinder prepared herself to be examined, I was reminded of her initial diagnosis of polycystic ovaries.

She was really very hairy indeed and came complete with quite an impressive moustache, gorilla like legs and an extraordinary pubic hair area, reminiscent of an Amazonian rain forest. I prepared myself for the rather daunting task of exploring her birth canal. Having fought myself through the undergrowth, I eventually found her cervix. A small blob of clear mucus was sucked out and placed on the microscopy slide. As usual, not a single sperm was seen down the microscope!

Caught in a Flap!

I returned to my desk and glanced at nervous-looking Terry. We listened to Lucy getting dressed and complaining about how difficult it was, given her weight, to get her continence knickers on. She also muttered something about her dentures and haemorrhoids playing up. I remember having a fleeting thought about whether these two problems may have been related!

The consultation continued and the current desperate state of affairs started to unravel itself, as I explained that there was no prospect of a pregnancy without sperms. Once again, I asked the couple whether intercourse was taking place regularly and without difficulty and once more they denied any problem. I looked at my patient again and momentarily reflected on how cruel nature was turning these enormous women into what looked like a fat, hairy bloke.

I then glanced at the diminutive figure of Terry, who was nervously fidgeting with his Train Spotters manual and looking uncomfortable in his green anorak. An evil thought crossed my mind about the realistic prospect of whether this couple were actually having sex.

"Do you mind if I have a private word with your husband Mrs Ballbinder?"

"What about?" she replied. "Man talk", I said somewhat unhelpfully. She reluctantly left.

"Mr Ballbinder, we need to talk man to man. There is clearly some kind of problem with these mysteriously vanishing sperms. I must ask, are you able to have proper sex with your wife, with your penis going deep into her vagina, leading to you ejaculating inside her? I really need to know."

There was a long pause as this little stick insect of a man looked penetratively into my eyes through his sellotape-repaired NHS spectacles.

"Would you shag that?"

Not a lot I could say to that I thought!

When I went home that afternoon, I started compiling my response to the inevitable complaint that was going to come through, regarding the management of this rather large patient. It didn't help knowing that many of the female managers in our directorate, who would be dealing with this complaint, had a similar body mass index and would probably view the situation from a slightly different vantage point!

Case 3—Rotveiller In The Pelvis!

One of the most tedious gynaecological consultations known to man is associated with the patient who has chronic, generalised, total body pain. These women play up thousands of gynaecologists across the world on a daily basis. The terrible thing about them is how they find their way into a gynaecological clinic in the first place. They all complain of pelvic pain initially.

This is usually associated with sexual pain which leads on to all sorts of other pains, involving every conceivable part of their body even their eyeballs! One can even tell what these patients are going to be like before they arrive in the clinic simply by looking at the referral letter from the GP. As a rule, in a state of desperation, the GP tries to focus on some kind of pain that can be related to a specialty in the hospital to which he can refer. Most women will finally associate their non-specific total body aches and pains to somewhere in their pelvis, if they are clever enough in manipulating their GP.

What starts as a bit of menstrual pain, pelvic penetration pain during intercourse, or ovulation pain, can soon find its way into the unwittingly naïve arena of the innocent gynaecologist. One such patient with total body ache (and total body pain for that matter) will always remain in my memory, as a deeply ingrained image of somebody that was totally unreal and outrageous and could easily have been the subject of a 'Hammer horror' film. Janice Blagthorne presented herself to my clinic as a forty-two year old gypsy woman.

To be politically correct I should call her a traveller, but nevertheless, she reminded me of one of those awful B-movie-style artists that would appear in dreadful eastern European films. You know; those films about travelling bands of circus people, who would flaunt their acts on the trapeze or perform with illegally imported elephants and bears.

Such people with no fixed abode would flit from one town to another, taking their wares, their acts and their entertainments with them. Janice Blagthorne looked just like one of those gypsies and in particular reminded me of one from an early James Bond film. I could easily imagine her doing a belly dance competition around a campfire, with loads of drooling Hungarians waiting to see which woman would win the catfight, just like in 'Dr No'! She had the evil look and the long bright red fingernails to match.

Unfortunately, she did not have the figure. Despite her tender age life had not been kind to her. In particular, the eight spontaneous vaginal deliveries from the age of fourteen did not help. The birth of these babies had certainly left their scars on her body. The poor woman was rife with varicose veins, stretch marks and very pendulous breasts. She wore extremely heavy belly-dancer style make up and had the most awful badly-dyed black hair, complete with bright white roots. To be completely frank, when she came into the consulting room I got quite a fright!

Nevertheless, I continued the consultation along the lines of what is expected from a respectable gynaecologist practising in the NHS, under the current regime of following good practice and political correctness. Incidentally, this regime takes nothing into account regarding the presentation of the patients, in terms of either frightening the living daylights out of their attendant physician or at best, just making the doctor feel completely intimidated or uncomfortable. This consultation was truly challenging on all of the above counts and I will try to describe it to you in detail. Ladies and gentlemen, I give you the story of the Rottweiller.

"Well Mrs Blagthorne, my name is Mr James and it's very nice to meet you. How can I help you today?"

"Well it's like this.Um like; I got this pain lower down."

"Alright, let's start from the beginning. How long have you had this pain for?"

"About 6 to 18 months", she said dryly.

"Would you like to tell me what brought it on in the first place?"

"I don't know really. It just sort of happened out of the blue."

"Would you like to describe the pain?" I asked rather lamely.

"Yeah, it feels deep down inside my fanny and hurts a lot." Grasping at straws I asked for a little more detail.

"Can you describe when this pain happens?"

"It can come at any time", she said. "It like, don't give no warning like and it can happen at any time of the day or night."

I started to feel that I was wading through treacle and decided to ask for some more detail, so that I could at least try to identify a possible diagnosis.

"Would you like to describe what this pain is like and what does it feel like to you?"

"Well", she said, "It feels like a Rottweiller." At this point I was on the verge of submission and ready to throw in the towel!

"Which part of a Rottweiller are we talking about?" (Hoping to God she wasn't going to mention its penis, or make any other reference to having sexual activities with an animal.) She looked at me with a glare and said, "Its facking teeth of course."

At this point I was desperate! I had to pursue the situation a little bit further. "You mean the Rottweiller is biting you from underneath?"

"Too bloody right", she said, "It's biting out my snatch and trying to tear my facking innards out."

Well, I thought that's at least a very graphic description of what's going on. Once again, I decided to do the honourable thing and start delay tactics! I asked her to give me a urine specimen to exclude infection and arranged the inevitable transvaginal scan to see what was going on in the pelvis. All this was done with a very reasonable six-week follow up appointment. Needless to say, Mrs Rottweiller was not happy with this consultation, as she wanted more clarification of the exact nature of her pelvic pain. I bade her good day and slumped back exhausted into my chair, with a cup of lukewarm tea that I'd been nursing throughout this consultation.

Case 4—Ginger Nut

Things were only going got get worse. The next woman to see me was also an albatross patient, almost in the same league as Mrs Blagthorne herself. This one, a fifty-two year old schizophrenic patient with three sons, all at various stages of the juvenile penitentiary system, not to mention her husband who was completely absent, was following me around with her longstanding history of vulval soreness and itchiness. I can truthfully say that I thought that I had done everything humanly possible to make a diagnosis for her uncomfortable undercarriage.

I had even taken her into the operating theatre and given her general anaesthetic so as to take loads of skin biopsies from the whole of her vulval, vaginal, perianal, periurethral and periclitoral areas, just to try and make a proper diagnosis. Short of sampling her tonsils I had tested everything! I prescribed every reasonable regime of emollient and cream that any dermatologist could imagine, but still I was getting absolutely nowhere.

Today's consultation was no different. I asked her how she'd been since the last course of treatment. Her reply was quite curt, "Since I'd been going through the mentalpause, I think the situation's getting worse." I tried to keep a straight face. "How do you know you're in the menopause?" I asked. She said, "Well I'm getting irritable and my itchiness has got a lot worse." Fair dues I thought, let's not prolong the agony. In desperation, I went on to my usual next move when I'm dealing with intractable disease for which I have not got a clue about what's going on. "Please may I examine you to see how the situation looks today?" I asked politely.

She willingly submitted herself to a formal clinical examination and promptly vanished behind the curtains. I followed with sister Lindy. We used a bright light to examine the condition of her nether regions. Once again, it was the usual story of a completely bald vulva with excessive vaginal discharge and a general redness of skin, which resembled a minor degree of sunburn, if one could imagine such a thing in that area.

Caught in a Flap!

Again I had to quiz her about what she was doing to her skin, given that she had promised me never to have any more baths or use soap in that area. She would never douche, use vaginal deodorants and never ever use Dettol!

"Are you sure you're not doing anything to irritate your skin?" I again queried.

"Absolutely certain", she said. "Doctor, I'm following all your instructions." I looked hard at the skin again in the glare of the bright light of the examination lamp.

"This area looks incredibly bald", I said. With a quizzical look on her face she said, "Of course it does doctor. I shave it five times a week with a Gillette G2 razor and Old Spice shaving foam." In stunned amazement I felt myself retort sarcastically, "Do you also put on aftershave, just to do a complete job?"

"Don't be stupid", she said, "That would cause irritation."

At this point, I could feel that I was losing the will to live in this clinic. I noticed it when Lindy had already vanished out of the door, probably to have a fit of hysterical laughter in front of the photocopier. In desperation, once again I asked her why she had to exfoliate herself to such an extreme level. She came out with the usual answer about feminine hygiene, which I have heard five trillions times before and then she had to take it one step further by bringing her family into the conversation. "Pubic hair is a nasty thing", she said, "It tells us that we are no longer children."

In stunned amazement, I had to ask her what possible relevance that was to her presentation. She continued regardless of my request and described in great detail how she walked into the bathroom quite recently, where her 15 year old son was languishing in the tub. "I was so surprised to see Gerald all covered with loads of ginger pubies. I realised at that moment that he had turned into a 'ginger nut' and my baby was gone forever." At this point I felt an overwhelming urge to throw up.

Chapter 30
Would You Like To Have Sex?

In gynaecological practice, there is always the risk that a consultation can go disastrously wrong, especially if you are addressing the rather delicate subject of sexual activity.

Unfortunately, our specialty attracts a lot of problems that are either directly or indirectly related to the acts of reproduction. On this occasion, I heard 'second-hand' through a very reliable source, about one of my colleagues, a very suave and beautifully dressed Mr Acropolis, who was obviously of Greek origin. Having been exported to the east end of London as a young child, he grew up and became a medical student at one of London's more prominent teaching hospitals. He had become much Anglicised and debonair and his good looks lent himself to being a very popular gynaecologist. Even in his late fifties, he cut a fine figure of a man and had a significant fan club of adoring nurses of all ages.

On this occasion, he was addressing the problem of pelvic floor prolapse in a woman in her late fifties. He had finished the consultation and examination and was leaning languidly against the wall with his left arm cocked behind his head in a rather casual fashion.

"You have a prolapse, Mrs Robinson", he said in his usual smooth drawl.

"Yes, I know doctor," she said.

"Does this affect you in any way?" he asked.

"Yes", she said, "It makes me feel a bit uncomfortable underneath."

"Do you have any trouble with your waterworks?" he asked.

"No, they seem to be reasonably alright", she said.

"Do you have sex?" he enquired.

"No, I don't", she said.

Caught in a Flap!

"Would you like to have sex?" he queried.

"Why, are you offering?" the patient asked quizzically.

The adoring nurse chaperone was found to wrap herself up in the consulting room curtains, as is so often the case when something very funny happens during a consultation.

Some months later, I was in the main theatres doing a combined list with Mr Acropolis and we both walked into the anaesthetic room to introduce ourselves to the patient, as is our usual good practice. The first patient on the list was for a vaginal repair to address the problem of prolapse. Mr Acropolis introduced himself and introduced me as well. The patient looked intensely into Mr Acropolis's eyes and said, "Oh, I remember you. You're the one who asked me if I wanted to have sex."

I looked appropriately shocked, turned and left the room in a purposeful manner, as if I was hot-footing it to find the first available telephone to contact the GMC immediately about this matter of gross misconduct.

Shortly afterwards Mr Acropolis left the anaesthetic room and returned to the theatre corridor. I looked at him in a grave and purposeful manner, trying to portray an air of concern compatible with impending 'whistle blowing' intentions. Unfortunately, I could not keep a straight face and I soon put him out of his misery by telling him that one of his admirers had told me, in great detail, about his original consultation with this patient.

I often wonder what would have happened if I had kept my mouth shut and continued to look shocked throughout the rest of the morning's list.

Chapter 31
No Matter What I Do

On a hot summer's afternoon, sitting in a terrible gynaecology clinic, a scraggy old duck comes in with her obese, middle-aged equally round scruffy-looking daughter. I went through my usual ritual of saying "Good afternoon, nice to see you, how are you?" (All completely insincerely of course) and then I got down to the nitty gritty of what the problem was.

I needed to know what was troubling this 67 year old school cleaner.

"Well", she said, in a broad cockney accent through her nicotine-stained teeth,

"It's a bit difficult for me to say this, so I've written it down on a piece of paper." She handed me a scruffy note so I put my glasses on and started to read. In spindly ball-point handwriting she described the following.

"No matter what I do, or what I say, or where I am, or where I go, if something brushes past my liquorice I will always have an organism".

By this time, I found it extremely hard to keep a straight face and I just wanted to burst into fits of hysterical laughter. I took a deep breath and looked at her seriously. "I think I'd better take you into the colposcopy room and examine the area that is worrying you."

Lindy, at this point, was frantically biting her lower lip and escorted the patient out and across the corridor into the colposcopy room. I joined them both a few minutes later. The old girl's legs were up in stirrups in the lithotomy position with her bottom appropriately positioned, just over the edge of the couch. I had my operating microscope ready and with perfect illumination I inspected her nether regions. I found no obvious evidence of disease and in particular, no evidence of skin irritation.

I picked up my Q-tip and told her that I was gently going to brush this cotton bud near the offending area. With my Q-tip carefully manipulated between finger and thumb, I aimed the cotton wool probe towards the clitoral hood. At that point, the woman started to shudder uncontrollably and exclaim loudly, "Oh no, 'ere we go again!" Her buttocks started to quiver like two giant jellies and the colposcopy stirrups began to creek in protest. At this point, Lindy ripped the Q-tip out of my hand, the examination promptly ceased and the orgasmic eruption rapidly subsided!

I did the honourable thing with this patient. I did what any well trained and conscientious consultant would do in such a situation. I referred her to a senior female spinster gynaecologist, who I was sure had more experience in this very difficult area!

As I finished dictating my letter, Lindy leaned over my shoulder and quietly whispered, "Whatever she is on, I want some!"

Chapter 32
Dangly Bits

One morning, as a consultant, I found myself in the operating theatre about to perform one of my more popular operations, called a labial reduction and vaginoplasty. I usually do these operations for women who are very worried about the size of their inner lips. The inner lips of the vulval area have an extraordinary variation in size from one woman to another. Some women have hardly any inner lips, just a simple, small ridge of tissue with a barely definable groove between that and the adjacent hairier large lip, called the labium majus.

As medical students, we always used to have a barrage of different terminologies to describe the female vulval region. In particular, if the woman had very prominent inner lips, a common descriptive terminology would be a 'bacon sandwich'! Particularly hairy vulvas were called 'fur burgers', and so on and so forth! I can even remember my youngest brother coining another descriptive phrase, following an unfortunate experience as a student in digs somewhere in Kingston.

On this particular occasion, there was a young redhead with extraordinary white skin, who generously apportioned her charms with several of the other lads who were sharing the house with her. One morning, this young lady, who had experienced a particularly busy night of sexual activity, had just got out of the bed next to my brother's and was bending over to pick up her knickers. Her bottom was right next to his face at the precise moment that he first opened his eyes. The combination of bright red vulval skin, matching pubic hair and of course pure white buttocks, led to some discussion amongst the lads in the pub later on at lunch time. PJ summed up the situation beautifully by saying, "Christ, as soon as I opened my eyes all I could see was this huge raspberry ripple!"

Continuing with my story . . . . vaginoplasty is a term used to describe how a vagina can be reconstructed to make it look neat again especially after the traumatic experiences of childbirth. I have already described in another chapter, my experiences of repairing the Irish woman who had just had a baby with a rather explosive delivery. In the operating theatre on this occasion, my brief was to reduce the lady's rather prominent lips, as well as to reconstruct the lower part of her vagina, which was disfigured and scarred following a very difficult forceps delivery, some six months previously.

I decided to do the labial reduction first, at which point the operating theatre's doors burst open and a long, lanky athletic-looking gynaecologist strolled purposefully towards my operating table. "Eeh Michael", he said in a broad Northern accent, "I've come to see one of your labial reductions. Our Lindy down in the outpatients' clinic says you're quite handy doing these and I'm curious to see what you get up to." "It's my pleasure to see you", I said lying through my teeth, "please come and watch". He came around to observe the operation site and thoughtfully studied the patient's vulval region.

After a brief pause he asked, "What's she 'avin done?" I answered "She'd like to have her lips reduced in size." He looked more purposefully at the vulva and then commented, "But they're not that big." So I said, "Well she finds them rather troublesome." "In what way?" he persisted. "Well, for a start, she finds them uncomfortable and they get caught in her underwear and press against her body. They get sore when she's wearing tight jeans and interrupt her ballet dancing when she's wearing a tutu", I replied.

Once again he paused thoughtfully and then announced in a foghorn voice, "Eeh Michael, if she 'ad what I've got dangling between my legs, then she'd have summ't to complain about!" I immediately took my gaze off the operating site and looked intensely into my consultant colleague's eyes. "I think I should tell you that this patient has an epidural and is awake". At that precise split second, I witnessed a fantastic impersonation of John Cleese from the famous TV series 'Faulty Towers', as my colleague bounced out of the operating theatre like a pogo stick, never to return in case his identity was revealed to my vulnerable patient.

To this day he doesn't know that she was really asleep!

Chapter 33
The Intrusive Husband

As far as I am concerned one of the world's greatest mistakes in the history of medicine, was the day they decided to invite husbands to watch childbirth. I have never personally been in favour of this particular visual feast. In fact it was only very recently that my dad told me it was a bit like being invited to watch your wife opening her bowels! The fact that bowel-opening often takes place coincidently with childbirth is neither here nor there! The trouble was that once watching childbirth became in vogue, it was only a matter of time before men started getting involved in gynaecological consultations!

Not long ago, as a consultant, I was asking a woman whether she was experiencing painful intercourse. She turned around to her husband and asked, "Fred, does it hurt when we make love?" I remember Fred looking as bemused and bewildered as I was. That's not the end of it. Try asking a woman whether she's having heavy periods and then she asks her husband the same question!

Where I really draw the line is when the husband feels that there is a need to come in and observe his wife's colposcopic examination. Ever since I can remember, I've always viewed a colposcopic examination of the vagina and cervix as a form of medical assessment and not a spectator sport to be enjoyed by the partner. Colposcopy involves inserting a metal speculum into the vagina and opening the two blades, so that one can see the cervix. A camera is then used in conjunction with a powerful microscope to examine the cervix and display an image of this organ on a television screen. Following that, an assessment is made which usually involves a repeat smear and/or a biopsy of some tissue from the cervix. It is not exactly 'rocket science', but for some reason many men are overwhelmingly interested in watching it.

On this particular occasion, I invited a 40 year old woman with three children to come in for her assessment. Her husband insisted on attending, saying that he always watched his wife's colposcopy.

Unfortunately, I was doing the clinic on behalf of another consultant so I had very little control of what was going on with regard to the husband's wishes. I, therefore, reluctantly agreed to allow him to watch the examination of his wife. I was nevertheless still irritable and rather fed up that I'd found myself in this situation, where I was breaking all the rules that I had been following for years as a colposcopist. In the back of my mind, I could not help feeling that there was emerging a sense of mischievousness against this over-demanding partner. I gently inserted a standard-sized speculum into the woman's vagina and started to look for the location of her cervix.

At that point, I could not help noticing that there were areas of slight skin-splitting in the vaginal skin. As I put the speculum a little further, the skin-splitting became more apparent as light bleeding was revealed. This was clearly an unusual finding, so I immediately asked the woman whether she had ever experienced bleeding in relation to sexual activity. Before she could even start to answer, the belligerent bricklayer husband chipped in saying that his wife always bled after 'he had given her a really good seeing to!'

Caught in a Flap!

My irritation with this man was escalating rather rapidly and I needed to stop his involvement as soon as possible. I turned around and looked him squarely in the eye. "Are you saying that every time you have intercourse your wife bleeds?" "Yes, that's it", he said proudly. I formulated a reply. "What I don't understand is that on today's examination I am using a particularly small speculum, which is only about two inches long and half an inch wide. What I am trying to say is, that it appears to me that very small objects inserted into your wife's vagina appear to be causing this bleeding and this is clearly rather unusual." I recall emphasising the word 'small' as I made this final comment.

At that point he got the message and said, "I'm going outside to read the paper. Cheers." Good riddance 'Needle Dick' I thought, as he scampered off into the waiting area with his 'page three girl newspaper' tucked under his arm.

If only I could deal with all the other 'spectator sport partners' the same way!

Chapter 34
Have You Got A Problem?

One day I found myself riding down to Cardiff on my beautiful grey Honda CBX motorcycle circa 1981. I was travelling to the annual British Society of Colposcopy and Cervical Pathology conference. I was quite excited about this trip, because I had a good paper to present and I thought it was going to be very well received by the delegates. I had booked into the Cardiff Thistle Hotel, which was meant to be a really comfortable establishment. I was making very good time until I took the wrong turning and ended up on the wrong slip road, which was going 35 miles south of Cardiff. As a result, I missed the opening ceremony at lunchtime and was very much miffed.

Nevertheless, I booked into my comfortable room and enjoyed the rest of the afternoon's intellectual entertainment. Traditionally at these conferences, groups of consultants would congregate together at various watering holes around the city where the conference was taking place. It is always a good opportunity to catch up with old pals and after many years of attending this particular scientific meeting, I have developed a close circle of drinking companions whom I only see once a year!

On this particular evening, after the conference, I found myself with the usual group of revellers, going from one public house to another and then attending the usual drinks get-together to celebrate the opening of the conference. This usually takes place in the town hall and often has a very good selection of red and white wines, as well as delicious canapés, all served by waitresses in little black skirts and white blouses.

After the reception, we invariably go on another pub crawl and more often than not the spree goes on until the early hours of the morning. On this particular occasion, I had the pleasure of the company of our colposcopy nurse Lindy and one of my colleagues from the department was also with us. Another one of my pals shocked us into complete disbelief during the drinking session, before we actually even had arrived at the reception. We were all in the hotel bar having a chat when this beautiful woman walked in towards the bar, 'half wearing' a black cocktail dress. This was a shoulderless, backless and strapless sort of number and she had lovely high-heeled shoes. Our friend Paul leapt off the settee that we were sitting on and gyrated towards the bar, where he promptly introduced himself.

In the distance, we could see him leaning on the bar with his elbows, whilst his bottom was waving around from side to side, as he obviously relished the anticipation of what delightful events could be occurring later in the evening. He appeared to be having a quiet drink with this young lady and after they had finished, they both vanished out of the bar not to be seen again for the rest of the evening. Lindy and I looked at each other in total disbelief. Had he arranged to see this woman through a dating agency? Was she an old friend? Was she a proper 'call girl', or was she something even naughtier? To this day, we have never found out and Paul has always kept very tight-lipped.

At the end of this very lovely evening, I found myself staggering back to the hotel. I made my way up to my room as normal and said "goodnight" to Lindy and I arranged to meet her for breakfast the following morning. I fell into a very deep sleep, only to be awoken at 3 am with this excruciating urge to have a huge pee. I staggered out of bed and made my way towards a door. I opened this door expecting to see that I was in the bathroom, but there was no toilet! I was in the corridor of the hotel and before I could turn round, I noticed the door silently click shut on its pneumatic arm. 'Oh God,' I thought, as soon as I realised that I was standing in a gloomy corridor with absolutely nothing on!

I was still dying for a pee. I frantically scrambled towards the door and realised immediately that there was no prospect of opening it as it was firmly shut. I started to panic. What would happen if someone saw me? I was meant to be giving a presentation the next day. What would happen to my reputation if some of the other delegates recognised me? I was beginning to feel decidedly unwell. I came up with an emergency contingency plan and frantically scurried up and down the corridor, hoping to find a laundry cupboard or something similar. I opened a door that did not look as if it belonged to a guest room and to my delight I discovered I was in a utility cupboard, full of packets of toilet rolls wrapped in clear plastic. In desperation, I opened one of these packets and unloaded 12 rolls of luxury toilet tissue. I examined the packaging and calculated that if I made two holes in the appropriate places, I could put my legs through them and make a nappy. I frantically did this and discovered that I had at least some semblance of a garment to wear!

As I staggered down the corridor, looking for the staircase that would lead me to the foyer of the hotel, I was acutely conscious of the fact that my nappy was totally transparent! Nevertheless, I continued down the stairs to the reception desk. In the dim light I could see a young youth-opportunities/work experience person doodling idly on his day planner. I walked over towards his desk, his gaze was still directed towards his work and he had not noticed me.

I coughed lamely and he looked up and took a sudden deep intake of startled breath. He rapidly composed himself and then asked as professionally as possible, "Do you have a problem Sir?" Quite shocked by his response, I could not help but exclaim in a rather loud and apprehensive manner, "Do I look like I've got a fucking problem?" Somewhat taken aback, he sniggered a little bit and then asked, "How can I help you then Sir?"

Caught in a Flap!

"I am locked out of my room wearing a transparent nappy", I said. "I can see that", he said, "Let's go up with the master key." "At last", I thought, "safely in the sanctuary of my room, but more importantly I can have a pee!" "Thank God", I thought to myself, "that nobody else has seen me." At that very point the rotating doors of the hotel started to move and a gaggle of night-time revellers staggered into the front foyer, all decidedly the worse for wear.

I recognised nearly every one as delegates of the conference and nearly died of embarrassment. I legged it up the stairs as quickly as I could, frantically dragging the receptionist with me. I eventually got to my room and was let in to have what felt like a 15-minute pee before going to bed. I woke up the next day thinking I'd had the most terrible nightmare about standing in the front foyer of a hotel with nothing but a transparent nappy around my nether regions!

Later on that day, I presented my paper and the Master of Ceremonies introduced me and said how refreshing it was to see me with some proper clothes on! Over lunch with Lindy, she quizzed me about what had happened the night before. I explained to her in agonising detail what had happened. "You are an idiot", she said, "Why didn't you just come and knock on my door and I would have sorted it all out."

I had this vision of myself standing outside Lindy's door at 3 am completely 'bollock naked' asking for some assistance. Somehow, I do not think that I would have got such an amicable response!

To this day, I still do not know what happened to my underpants!

Chapter 35
And Finally . . .

I find myself sitting in a dreary colposcopy clinic in a gloomy room with no windows, somewhere in the south east of London. The miserable female patient sitting in front of me has a face as long as a horse. Sound familiar? The trouble with this situation is that I realise that it has been five years since I wrote the first line of this book. It suddenly occurs to me that nothing has changed! Here I am, once again, sitting in front of a disgruntled patient, who's clearly fed up with her whole clinical situation and there is very little that I can do to improve her lot.

Today's patient has had repeated abnormal smears and keeps coming back to the colposcopy clinic because they never get better. I have told her over and over again, that smoking 40 cigarettes a day is a guaranteed way of making sure that the abnormal cells do not clear up on their own. This is the fifth time she has come back and this is the fifth time I have explained that if she continues to smoke, the abnormal cells will not go.

Do you think she can grasp this concept? The answer is clearly 'No'. Instead, she just gets angry with me for not being able to make the disease go away. I swear to God that if I hear her say once more, just once more; "All my friends and family smoke and there's nothing wrong with their front bottoms", then I'm certain I'll commit an act of violence, either towards myself or towards her, with very little prospect of restraining myself! Why is this situation making me feel so agitated?

Why do I get so angry at work on a daily basis? Why does it only take a matter of minutes after arriving at the hospital, before something happens to make me truly irritated? Why am I turning into such a grumpy old man?

The smoking patient leaves my clinic, with the assurance that she will do everything to give it up and come back again in six months, hopefully to find herself with a normal smear. Later on as I leave the clinic, I see her quietly lighting up in the car park before driving off, having just dumped a whole ashtray full of cigarette butts all over the pavement. "God give me strength", I mutter to myself, as I walk towards my motorcycle.

Caught in a Flap!

That evening when I got home, I found myself in an unusual position, because the house was empty. The girls were out having extra lessons and piano practice and my wife was doing a late clinic. I found myself sitting quietly in my study with a glass of wine, reflecting on my current situation. I thought "Was it really so bad; was the Health Service going downhill as badly as I thought, or was it just my imagination, because I'd had a recent bad patch at work?"

I decided to reflect on the previous week and look at the good things and the bad things and make a sensible judgement about what my true predicament was really like. I drew up a plain piece of paper with a dividing line down the middle. On the left, I was going to write the good things that had happened to me and on the right; I was going to put down all the bad things that had happened during the previous seven days. To try and drive myself with a certain air of optimism, I decided to do the good things first, rather than concentrate on the bad things.

After sitting there for nearly 20 minutes, I still hadn't written anything down on the good side and then I remembered something which cheered me up. One of the 'top dog' consultants at a leading teaching hospital 'tertiary referral centre' had written a letter back to me saying that the quality of my referral, the clarity of my surgical diagrams and my accurate diagnosis on this young girl's congenital condition, could only be described as 'exemplary'. I felt a quiet moment, albeit briefly, of satisfaction.

Spurred on by this transient wave of enthusiasm I franticly tried to think of another pleasant event. I suddenly remembered the vision of our lovely au pair standing in front of her bedroom window completely naked on a dark winter's afternoon. I had been walking five year old Susan back from school and realised that all the tall trees lining our front fence had been cut back from the house. Leila had not noticed this and, as usual, had not drawn the curtains. The added bonus was that she was standing in front of a full length mirror whilst she leisurely brushed her long black hair. Nothing was left to my imagination as I admired this spectacle. After about 10 minutes I felt Susan tug my hand and ask if she could go inside now as she was feeling very cold!

As this lovely image faded I found myself once again looking at the column of bad things. I thought about the morning when I had arrived at work, only to find the entire front entrance area of the hospital splattered with literally thousands of discarded cigarette butts. There were forlorn-looking patients and relatives standing outside the front door of the hospital, all lighting up.

Behind them, only a few feet away, were huge hospital signs telling us that we were not allowed to smoke anywhere in the hospital or grounds. Some of these signs were as high as eight feet tall stating, "If you're thinking of lighting up, don't!" I saw a man standing in a string vest and scruffy corduroy trousers with a cigarette hanging out of his mouth. He was standing right next to the front sliding-door of the hospital and as I approached, he blew a big plume of smoke into my face.

"Excuse me sir", I said as politely as my irritation would allow, "You do realise that smoking is not allowed anywhere on the hospital premises." Before I could finish my sentence he retorted, "Fuck off you fat cunt!"

"Charming", I thought, as I walked through the sliding door into the entrance foyer. Fed up and disappointed at my lack of success in trying to amend the ways of 'Joe Public', I shared my experience with a sharp-witted surgical colleague who was climbing the same staircase as me. After I'd told him what had happened, he said, "Mikey, but you're not fat." I had to see the humour in his comment.

I proceeded to my clinic via my secretary's office to find out whether the patients for my special bereavement clinic had booked in. I had been running this clinic for many years and it has been used exclusively to see patients who have had traumatic or upsetting experiences, such as losing their babies, or having disastrous outcomes from their surgical procedures.

At best, these consultations can be described as miserable and at worst, agonising. They can sometimes go on for hours and one finds oneself in a situation, usually where the whole consultation has been devoted to offering apologies to the couple, on behalf of the hospital and other individuals. As I approached the bereavement room, where the consultation was about to take place, I expressed to my clinic sister once again, how fed up I was of always having to apologise for other people.

Caught in a Flap!

The first thing that struck me about this consultation was that, curiously, I did not recognise the woman in front of me, or her partner. I was already starting to get quite anxious that I may not be very familiar with their set of circumstances, in which case, the whole consultation would be further compromised. I anxiously flicked through the notes, having offered my introduction and found, to my total bewilderment, that this woman was never booked under my care and I'd never had any clinical contact with her.

I felt an overwhelming urge to kill anybody who was involved in making this ridiculous appointment. The poor woman and her partner had cancelled their holidays and driven all the way down the motorway, some 200 miles, to see me especially to discuss the circumstances of their recent stillbirth. Can you imagine how it felt to try and explain to them this terrible gaff?

Nevertheless, I proceeded with the consultation, even though I didn't know her from 'Adam' and tried to make the very best of it, given the ridiculous error that had taken place. Needless to say, I was never able to find out who was responsible for this ludicrous situation and no doubt I never will.

I went to my operating list in the afternoon and found out that there were no junior doctors available, not even a GP trainee SHO to help me do major surgery. I tried to ring the consultant in charge of the juniors' allocation and found that he was on annual leave. I went to the consultants' rest room in theatres and found a general surgeon in exactly the same predicament, frantically phoning around all the juniors and literally pleading for help. What a far cry from those early days, when the SHO would arrive in theatre first and present all the cases to the consultant, before the list had even started.

After operating, I went to look at my e-mails and found yet another barrage of complete drivel appearing on the screen. One of the consultants was proposing that we provide a list of which consultants on the 'on-call' rota can get to the hospital in the shortest possible time for any emergency. Presumably, this means you could call that consultant whether he was on duty or not, just because he happens to live close to the hospital.

My name was mentioned because I have a very high performance motorcycle, which obviously trims the journey time considerably. I responded to this notion by stating, quite clearly, that I wanted everyone to know, "When I am not on duty, I am well over the drink/drive limit until proved otherwise!"

Another e-mail was welcoming me to the Deanery training session for managing junior doctors' educational requirements. I was required to prepare an essay and a whole raft of other tasks involving filling in forms, but there was one slight problem; the date of the meeting had been finalised for the following morning! There was no way I would be ready and it was too late to send my cancellation notification. "Oh bollocks . . . . !"

There was even a non-medical e-mail on the computer screen to cause me more irritation. This one was about an incident involving my boat over in a Surrey marina. A few months previously, I had come into the lock, which was rather full of vessels and I brushed alongside a brand new boat called 'Memory Creator', the fender of which fell off in the lock.

This resulted in a tiny scratch near the stern of the boat, where my rubbing rail had brushed past her gel coat. The fat owner had spotted this injury to his vessel and pointed it out to me afterwards. I had agreed to get it fixed at the end of the season, just before his boat went into storage. We had shaken hands and agreed on this arrangement. I was therefore appalled to find that on the e-mail he had changed his mind and had reported me to the marina manager for negligent handling of my boat. He also wanted to report me to the lock keeper and of course to my insurance company.

All this was contrary to the arrangements that we had shaken hands on and I was absolutely incandescent with rage. To make things even worse, he came out with a 'one-liner', which I will never forget. This particular part of the message had been addressed to the Director of Marina Services and described how he had to "endure a whole six months cruising around the coast of England in a scratched boat, which was a result of Dr James' negligence".

I read the e-mail and exclaimed in a loud voice, "Fat spoilt bastard!" I immediately responded to the director by stating that if all my ill patients, particularly those with cancer, had 'only' to endure cruising around the coast of England in a scratched boat, then they would no doubt be very grateful for their lot.

CAUGHT IN A FLAP!

I expressed that I would be looking forward to seeing 'Mr Phat Buoy' in the small claims court, so that we could discuss the matter of the miniscule scratch on 'Mammary Creator'. After all he was such a 'tit'!

I was irritated when I left my computer and proceeded to the surgical ward to see an emergency admission that I had looked after over the weekend. On arriving at the nursing station, needless to say, there were no nurses to attend me and I sat there looking at the patient admission board for the next ten or so minutes, just twiddling my thumbs and getting more and more agitated. Eventually, a disinterested-looking staff nurse meandered over towards the desk and asked me if I needed anything.

At that point, a gentleman in his late 40s, wearing only a pair of pyjama bottoms with his genital region clearly exposed through an open fly, waddled down the corridor topless, catheterised and not even wearing a pair of slippers! The whole situation was reminiscent of a refugee camp and I politely asked the staff nurse whether there were any standards pertaining to a dress code for male patients on a mixed ward. She shrugged her shoulders and grunted.

After seeing the aforementioned patient, I made my way down to the hospital staff car park, only to find my air pager alerting me to a call. It was the day-surgery unit calling to say that none of the patients I had operated on had been discharged, as the only junior doctor who had been around had gone off early without notice. The registrar was too busy in theatre and the patients needed to have their discharge letters done. I reluctantly agreed to come back to the day-care unit fuming and swearing all the way back up the hospital car park steps.

The husband of the first patient I needed to see greets me with "Watcha mate", as I made my way through the curtains. I then got embroiled in a very difficult argument about how his wife could have possibly developed huge genital warts, when she was the only person that he had ever slept with etc! Not a lot I could say to that, I thought at the time!

The next woman I needed to discharge was absolutely livid that her operation was cancelled by the registrar, because he'd gone into theatre and decided that she was 'Virgo intacta', and therefore, could not have a gynaecological operation in her vagina. On reading my clinic notes, I had quite clearly stated that this woman's hymen could be disrupted during the surgery to facilitate entry into the uterus, as long as it was repaired and reconstituted with a few stitches afterwards. Needless to say, the registrar had not read any of my correspondence and had made a complete balls-up of this woman's entire procedure, leaving me to apologise!

Eventually, I escaped from the day-care unit and at last I could see the silhouette of my car in the distance. As I approached the barrier of the car park ready to make my escape, I once again bumped into the sister in charge of the gynaecology clinic. Her electric window came down slowly and she looked rather hesitantly at me over the barrier. "What's the matter?" I asked. She looked rather awkwardly at me and said "You do know that your registrar isn't in clinic tomorrow, because he's attempting the Membership examination for the 10th time at the Royal College?"

"Yes" I said, "I knew he was going". "Well, unfortunately", she said, "You're not gonna like this". "Go on", I said. "Well someone forgot to reduce your clinic and they've got 25 patients ready for you tomorrow afternoon. Do you have a short operating list in the morning?" "No", I said, desperately trying to hold back expletives and deletives. "I've already agreed to do three extra cases to help with the waiting list." I wound my window up and once again found myself saying, "Oh bollocks!"

So, going back to the right-hand side of my paper, not only have I been able to fill up the column on the front, I have also filled it up in its entirety on the back. On the left-hand side, with good things happening, I have recorded just the two entries.

I left my study and went downstairs to sit outside our little cottage to admire our chickens, which, because of the fox, can only come out when there is an adult to supervise them. I recharge my glass and once again ponder my current situation. "It can't be all that bad surely?" I decided to think about the good, positive things outside my work in medicine. I thought about my family life, my homes and with some pleasure, about my collection of vehicles, which I have been devoted to over the last 25 years or more. In particular, I relished the idea of my Porsche 911 Carrera 4. I had always wanted one of these vehicles.

Caught in a Flap!

Recently, I had been steaming drunk during a holiday in Germany, while staying at my sister-in-law's and found myself the worst for wear after a session on German yeast beer. I plugged myself into eBay and despite 'seeing double' on the screen, ended up buying a Porsche! There is not enough space or time to describe the repercussions that occurred when my wife found out about this purchase, but suffice to say at the end of day, I was thrilled with it.

I suddenly realised that my front garden had to be evacuated of all the vehicles, so the tree surgeons could come round. I picked up my glass of wine and decided to walk outside and make sure the Porsche was alright. I had parked it in a neighbour's drive round the corner to avoid the falling trees. On arriving at his driveway, I was amazed to find that my beautiful car was covered in vomit, both on the windscreen and entire rear window. Apparently, some charming teenage yobs decided they needed to throw up all over my car! Their acidic vodka and ale-tainted vomitus was already starting to dissolve the paint! Maybe my social circumstances weren't so marvellous after all.

I thought about the new Suzuki Hayabusa that had been stolen outside my front door a few months earlier and of course the theft of the another identical Suzuki in the village only a few months before that. I developed this overwhelming desire to get the hell out of this whole situation. I needed to move and change my job. All of a sudden, my imagination started to run riot.

Maybe I could emigrate to New Zealand and start a whole new life there. Maybe I could stop doing operative gynaecology and just do straightforward clinical work in a locum setting. Maybe I could just do two or three clinical sessions a week, play the role of a house husband and ask my wife to do extra sessions in her job. All of these marvellous plans would rely on us spending less money and cutting back in some way; but I would be happier, under less strain and enjoying my life again.

As I lay in bed that night, these thoughts were churning over in my mind. I remembered the words of a friend from school in Africa, whom I saw in New Zealand quite recently, after he'd changed his career as a successful consultant anaesthetist to become a sheep farmer in New Zealand. He told me that he'd made the decision at a certain point in his life before it was too late. He thought that point in his life should be well before he was 50. At the time of our conversation he'd just reached 50 and was on a farm with 6,000 sheep on the South Island of New Zealand.

The weather was freezing and bleak and I couldn't understand how he could possibly be enjoying himself, but he was. What a brave bloke, I thought, to make such a monumental life-changing decision. And how funny it was to think that his Dutch surname 'Scharp' meant sheep!

Did I think I had the balls to do it myself? Probably not, because none of these thoughts appeared to be stopping my seriously drooping eyelids.

As I battled with my eyelids I pondered over lots of things that I had written about in this book. I thought about what it has been like to be a gynaecologist and all my funny friends in Africa with their marvellous names, such as 'Cathy Balls Anus' and 'Sparrowfart'. I also thought about all the naughty things that I had done, particularly to other people and all that others had done to me!

As I finally drifted off to sleep, I was left with a fading, but hilarious image of my friend Andy, explaining to Helen why he wanted an 'amster to keep on his camp bed for company after she'd left him.

Or was that an Alsatian?

About This Book

For those of you adult readers who have ever wondered about what it would be like to aspire to become a gynaecologist, well now is your chance to find out!

Desmond Parunia, in writing 'Caught in a Flap', tells a story seen through the eyes of a young schoolboy, Mikey.

Mikey who emigrated to sunny Rhodesia in the late sixties, becomes fascinated by the mystery of female anatomy after spending most of his free time frolicking in swimming pools surrounded by bikini-clad beauties. Having only two brothers and no sisters only added to the intrigue! ***Nothing like this ever happened at Epsom Baths!***

Desmond takes us through the frustration and excitement of a young man growing up in a world where there appeared to be an endless supply of new experiences. A world where one was about to discover rude films, pop music, stereo Hi Fi, candy-coloured super fast Japanese motorcycles, driving cars, drinking beer and of course . . . . girls! Mikey has a reasonable shot at most of the material things, but the girls remain elusive, particularly from the point of revealing their dark secret! In desperation, Mikey tries to impress them with his ambition to become a gynaecologist. The story then goes on to unravel a disjointed and sometimes hilarious escapade of life sketches capturing mainly the highs but sometimes the lows of what it was really like fulfilling that ambition.

Please note that the author does **not** recommend you reading this book to your children at bed time!

Disclaimer

None of the patients described in this book exist and the names of health care professionals have been changed for obvious reasons.

Dedication

This book is dedicated to those parents who put so much extra effort into their less-gifted (thick?) offspring to get them through their 'A' levels and then on to university. Without all the extra coaching and help with homework, as well as financial support to re-sit so many examinations, I know that I would never have ended up 'looking up' what I do today!

Printed in Great Britain
by Amazon.co.uk, Ltd.,
Marston Gate.